D0238340

.99

/08

Prue Leith divides her time between her School of Food and Wine, her party-catering company and Leith's, her prestigious London restaurant. Her cookbooks, cookery articles and demonstrations have inspired cooks throughout the world to impress their guests with a minimum of fuss and time spent in the kitchen. Her successful *Cook's Handbook* is also available in Papermac.

Prue Leith's Dinner Parties

Illustrations by Vivien Ashley

PAPERMAC

First published in Great Britain 1984 by Robert Hale Limited:
a Jill Norman book

First published in paperback 1985 by
PAPERMAC
a division of Macmillan Publishers Limited
4 Little Essex Street, London WC2R 3LF
and Basingstoke

Associated companies in Auckland, Delhi, Dublin, Gaborone,
Hamburg, Harare, Hong Kong, Johannesburg, Kuala Lumpur, Lagos,
Manzini, Melbourne, Mexico City, Nairobi, New York, Singapore
and Tokyo

Reprinted 1986, 1987, 1990, 1991

British Library Cataloguing in Publication Data

Leith, Prudence
Prue Leith's dinner parties.
1. Dinners and dining
I. Title
641.5'68   TX737

ISBN 0-333-39308-2

Photoset by Rowland Phototypesetting Limited

Printed in Hong Kong

The author would like to thank Jane Lunzer
for her great help in what was often an exacting and
laborious job – checking, typing, editing and testing.

CONTENTS

INTRODUCTION

The ambition of a dinner party host should be to have the guests departing extremely reluctantly, later than they should, but feeling great – not over-fed, exhausted or not-quite-sober.

The trick is not, as one might expect, to be mean with the drink, but rather to be very careful with the food. It is the combination of too much rich food and alcohol that is responsible for that inner groan the morning after. Even if you do not drink at all, you can be horribly hung-over after a meal consisting of taramasalata, roast pork, ratatouille and crème brûlée. It may not be obvious to the diner, but all those dishes contain a much higher than average amount of fat. If they are delicious, and especially if the hostess is pressing him to second and third helpings, the guest is going to subject his poor liver to such a lambasting that the next day is bound to be a penance.

Of course that is not to say you should cut out, in a dedicated and humourless spirit, everything that is any fun to eat. Just serve it in elegantly small quantities, with relaxed gaps between courses (which is better for conversation anyway), and make sure the menu is balanced. Cream, alcohol, or eggs should not appear in every course – a meal of omelettes, followed by something in mayonnaise, followed by a cold soufflé can mean one person unwittingly eating five eggs at a sitting.

This book follows the traditional pattern of first course, main course, pudding. But naturally, three courses are not obligatory. Two will very often do better. Or you may prefer to serve four or five, à la française, with a salad or a single vegetable forming a separate course, and follow with a bite of cheese. But if this is to be, each course must consist of tiny portions. Serving a lot of small courses makes for a lot of washing up, but is in fact a good way to eat lightly, mainly because the numerous courses take time to serve and appetite is largely assuaged ten minutes after the first mouthful. Convention generally demands

1

that we eat most of what is on our plates. If what is on our plates is very little, we take a long time over it, and our stomachs are soon fooled into non-hunger. If we are given a great mound of food (albeit only a single course) we can get through an awful lot before ten minutes is up.

About the drink: it is a truism that good booze leaves you feeling better than bad booze. It is also true that a bottle of wine drunk slowly over a very long period is better than three gin-and-tonics before dinner, half a bottle of red during, and port or brandy to follow. It is not of course possible to control the guests' drink to the same degree as their food. But there is no need to ply people with wine, topping up glasses at every sip. It is much better to put the bottle on the table, and not worry too much if someone's glass is empty for a few minutes. Anyone who really wants a glass badly will reach for the bottle, and someone who wants to go easy won't feel a killjoy, constantly having to get his or her hand over the glass before the nippy host has filled it up.

The modern fashion for arranging food on individual plates has many advantages, though it generally means more work for the cook and needs shelf upon shelf of refrigeration space. The advantages are that a small amount of food can be made to look wonderfully appetising, and that the cook knows exactly how much to prepare (no danger of someone helping himself to double helpings or, which is more usual, a good half of the dish being left over). Also, prettily arranged first and last courses do elicit suitable gasps of admiration from the audience. But for the home cook to follow the restaurant practice of elegantly dishing up the main course, placed exactly on its perfect lake of sauce, with tiny spoons of vegetables all round, is frankly impracticable without a brigade of experienced chefs in the kitchen. I would recommend sticking to the traditional method – the meat on one large platter, vegetables or salad in a second dish or bowl. But the host or carver should make sure helpings are neat and attractive on the plate.

I do not think it necessary, or desirable, to have potatoes, rice, noodles or something starchy at every meal. A single green vegetable or a salad is often preferable. And one vegetable, or at the most two, is enough. Trying to reheat or cook three green vegetables and potatoes at the last minute is bound to mean a hot and bothered cook, if not cool and overdone vegetables.

I have made suggestions for vegetables or salads to go with every menu, but obviously peas could be swopped for beans, carrots for turnips, cabbage for sprouts or rice for mashed potato. The essential

:hing is to provide a contrast. If you are serving stew, which is essentially soft, brown and wet, you need a crisp and green contrast (say spring cabbage or Chinese leaves) and rice or potatoes to mop up the sauce. Ratatouille, which is brown, soft and wet too, would not be good.

Only superwomen or the romantic male lead in the movies can whisk up dinner while the guests stand round the kitchen, glass in hand. In real life the best dinner parties are the ones with the best-laid plans. I unashamedly make lists and stick them on the refrigerator door, so that, even after a couple of drinks, I can move through the last minute routine, 'take salad out of fridge', 'add pine-nuts to casserole', 'melt chocolate sauce', etc. without having to think. If I omit these pedantic precautions I discover the uneaten salad when I'm washing up, or find the chocolate sauce still frozen while the ice cream is melting fast.

If everything that can be done in advance is done in advance, the table laid, the towels in the bathroom changed, the flowers arranged and the coffee things set out, it is surprising how often even the working cook/host with two hours between getting home and blast-off can get a twenty-minute soak in the bath too. Menus that can be prepared ahead of time are listed on page 4.

The main thing to remember about having people to dinner is that your friends are coming to see you, not to award rosettes for gastronomic skills. They will have a better time if you are relaxed, happy and part of the party, rather than a flushed and anxious supernumerary turning out complicated gastronomic creations. 'Keep it simple' is such an old cliché I hesitate to use it, but nothing in the past twenty years has happened to make me think the British cook has got the message.

It is a most rare and wonderful treat to get a straightforward dinner of, say, tomato salad, roast lamb and gooseberry fool. Indeed, I suppose I could be accused, with some justice, of making the menus in this book too complicated, but I am in this difficulty – I can hardly write a cookbook where half the starters and half the desserts require no cooking: plain melon or avocado to start, cheese or a perfect peach to finish. So the menus, though I trust they are well balanced, are intended for the cook who likes cooking, and can make the time to do it. But I should regard the substitution of a creamy piece of Stilton, or a bowl of perfect cherries, as thoroughly sensible for anyone who does not want to cook three courses. All menus serve 8 people.

3

Menus that can be ninety-percent prepared ahead of time
1, 6, 8, 9, 10, 11, 14, 15, 17, 19, 21, 24, 27, 29, 31, 32, 33, 34, 35, 36, 37, 39, 40, 41, 42, 43, 45, 48, 50, 51.

Wine

On the subject of wine: most people, simply and perfectly reasonably, go for dry red or dry white with all meals from hot curries to delicate fish dishes, with the old adage 'white with fish and red with everything else except pudding' to guide them. There is nothing wrong with such an attitude, but it is important that the standard white or standard red is sound and drinkable. For anyone who genuinely likes wine, never mind for the true wine-lover or connoisseur, it is perfect agony to be offered bad wine. One cannot swallow the stuff, and to ask the host to swop it for beer or water is impossibly insulting. Good wine does not have to be expensive and for those readers not particularly interested in wine, or unable to spend time and money tasting their way through unknown bottles at the wine-merchants, I would advise trusting someone with a reputation to lose such as Marks and Spencer, Harrods, Sainsbury, Peter Dominic or Victoria Wine: all will have their own 'House' red and white, and as they sell more of this than of more expensive wines, they cannot afford for it to be unreliable or nasty.

Wine, once one starts to learn a bit about it, is fascinating, and for many people it becomes an engrossing obsession. Much can be learnt from books provided reading goes hand in hand with tasting and drinking. Time-Life's book, *Wine*, in the Good Cook series is excellent, as is Jancis Robinson's *The Wine Book*.

But should you neither want to embark on a thorough wine education, nor confine your drinking to House red and House white, perhaps the following remarks may prove helpful:

There are of course conventional marriages of wine and food, and it is sensible, if in doubt, to stick to the conventions. But only the most ignorant and pompous wine snob would pretend that there is only one perfect wine for a particular dish.

I have drunk, against the rule of light and simple wines with light and simple food, huge complex and expensive white Burgundy (a Montrachet no less) with freshly cooked shrimps from a market stall. Both tasted wonderful. But it would be more usual, and certainly more sensible, to save such wine treasures for grander occasions than

4

shrimps on the seafront. Frankly I think that whether you serve expensive and wonderful wine, or simple wholesome plonk, is more a matter of who you are dining with than what you are dining on. There is absolutely no point in pulling out your best bottle for someone whose favourite tipple is Wincarnis, or for a confirmed beer and whisky man. There is every point in giving the best to friends who will appreciate it.

The English convention is, very roughly, dry white wine with the first course, dry red wine with the main course, especially if it consists of a meat or poultry dish. If the main course is fish a grander (and therefore heavier, fuller, more complex) white wine than the one served with the first course would generally replace the red. Dessert is accompanied, if at all, by a sweet wine or a champagne. Port, or more red wine, is served with the cheese. If serving cheese and pudding, it is sometimes wise to follow the French habit of cheese-before-pud, which allows one to keep drinking the red, uninterrupted by the sweet course. Sweet wines with savoury dishes are a mistake. They deaden the appetite and are rather unpleasant – like eating jam sauce with fish. There is a fashion at the moment (adopted from the French who, to English eyes, appear to drink anything with anything) for drinking dessert wine as an aperitif or to accompany foie gras – that seems to me a millionaire's recipe for migraine.

But to continue with the English conventions. Really sweet dessert wine is served only with pudding, though German-style wines made elsewhere from the same grapes (Riesling, Sylvaner, Traminer), provided they are no sweeter than the Spätlese grade, are good with savoury dishes too. Medium or dry, never sweet, sherry is sometimes served with soup, beer with curry, champagne or vodka with caviar.

So much for the Dos. What about the Don'ts?

Some people, to my mind rather pompously, refuse to serve wine with a dish containing lemon or vinegar on the grounds that the acidity spoils the wine. True, but why cannot one have a mouthful of bread to separate the two? Or serve a wine, such as a white Loire, with enough acidity of its own to stand up?

I do think it a mistake to serve red wine, unless it is very light and not at all tannic, with fish. Well-flavoured claret will give fish an unpleasantly metallic taste.

Overpoweringly strong tastes like curry and other spicy Eastern foods so overshadow subtle, expensive wines that it is a waste of money to serve them. Good, robust, powerful Spanish or South African wine would be better.

On the question of vintages: a vintage chart, which tells you which areas made good and bad wine in recent years, is useful, but not infallible. As a rule it is better to spend money on a less well-known wine of a good year than on a great name in a bad year. The further south one goes – the Rhône, Spain, Italy, and in the 'new' wine areas – California, Chile, South Africa and Australia – the less do vintages matter: the weather is generally reliably hot and the wine correspondingly uniform.

MENU 1

GAZPACHO
DAUBE À LA PROVENÇALE
VACHERIN WITH BANANAS
AND GRAPES

Introduction
It is sometimes sensible to hedge one's bets on the weather by serving an iced summer soup with a warming hotpot to follow.

Cook's gear
A processor or liquidizer for the soup.

Two baking trays and greaseproof paper for the vacherin; piping bag with a large nozzle (optional).

Cook's tips
Ensure that the soup is well refrigerated if made in advance as it ferments fast in warm surroundings.

To remove fat easily from daube sauce, either chill it until the fat solidifies (stand the casserole in a bowl set in the sink and run constant cold water into the bowl; this will quickly chill the casserole and its contents), or spoon off what you can and then lay successive sheets of absorbent paper on the surface of the liquid, lifting them off as they absorb the fat.

When peeling tomatoes, dip them in boiling water for five seconds to loosen skins.

To achieve perfectly shaped vacherins, use a flan ring or cake tin to mark 20cm/8in circles in the oil-and-sugar coating on the greaseproof paper, then pipe or spoon the meringue within the confines of the circles.

Bananas and grapes are a good combination of rich-textured and fresh-tasting fruit, but other mixtures are good too – cherries, raspberries and redcurrants, or pineapple, dates and walnuts.

Getting ahead

Make soup and croûtons the day before; refrigerate soup; store croûtons in airtight container.

Marinate beef and vegetables for the daube up to 48 hours ahead. Cook the day before. Keep refrigerated.

The meringue discs can be made well in advance and stored in an airtight container. Prepare fruit four hours before and assemble one hour before dinner.

Vegetable or salad?

Serve something absorbent like mashed potatoes, rice or noodles to mop up the sauce. Forget green vegetables or salads if you like – the gazpacho provides raw vegetables, plenty of colour and abundant vitamin C.

Gazpacho

2 slices white bread, without
   crusts
2 egg yolks
2 large cloves garlic
150ml ¼pt olive oil
2tbsp tarragon vinegar
750g 1½lb fresh, very ripe
   tomatoes, skinned
lkg 2lb tinned Italian peeled
   tomatoes

2tbsp tomato purée
3 red peppers, seeded and
   chopped
1 large, mild-tasting onion,
   chopped
1 cucumber, peeled and
   chopped
rock or sea salt
freshly ground black pepper

To serve
1 small bowl of each of the
   following:
   diced cucumber
   diced green and red pepper
     mixed

skinned diced tomatoes
chopped raw mild onion
small fried croûtons

1 Liquidize bread, egg yolks and peeled garlic until smooth.
2 Add oil in steady stream to produce a mayonnaise-like emulsion.
3 Add vinegar. Tip into bowl.
4 Liquidize remaining ingredients.
5 Add to mixture in bowl. Stir. Taste. Chill.
6 Serve ice-cold with diced vegetables and croûtons.

Daube à la Provençale

2kg   4lb chuck steak
2 large onions, sliced
3 large carrots, sliced
2 cloves garlic, chopped
1 bouquet garni: bay leaf,
   parsley sprigs, thyme, celery
   stick, tied together
4tbsp olive oil

¾ bottle red wine
salt and pepper
250g   8oz unsmoked streaky
   bacon, thickly sliced
350g   12oz tomatoes
300ml   ½pt good stock
12 black olives, stoned

1 Cube beef.
2 Marinate for 24 hours with vegetables, garlic, bouquet garni, oil, wine, salt and pepper.
3 Next day: set oven to 150°C/300°F/Mark 2.
4 Line bottom of casserole with bacon strips.
5 Add marinated ingredients and liquid, skinned quartered tomatoes and stock.
6 Bring to boil. Cover tightly. Put in oven for 4 hours, or until very tender.
7 Lift out meat and vegetables into clean, flameproof dish, removing bouquet garni.
8 Skim fat off liquid. Check seasoning and add olives.
9 Pour over meat, reheat and serve.

Vacherin with Bananas and Grapes

6 egg whites
350g   12oz caster sugar
2 bananas
lemon juice
100g   4oz black grapes

100g   4oz green grapes
450ml   ¾pt double cream,
   lightly whipped
icing sugar

1 Set oven to 100°C/200°F/Mark 1/2
2 Line two baking sheets with greaseproof paper. Brush with oil and dust with caster sugar.
3 Whisk egg whites until stiff.
4 Add 2 tablespoons sugar. Whisk until very stiff and shiny.
5 Fold in remaining sugar.
6 Pipe or spoon meringue into two flat 20cm/8in rounds.
7 Bake 2–3 hours, or until the paper can be easily peeled from the meringue.

8 Peel bananas, cut into chunks and toss in lemon juice.
9 Halve and seed the grapes.
10 Spread one meringue case with the cream. Scatter over the banana and grapes.
11 Place second meringue case on top. Dust with icing sugar.

MENU 2

JAPANESE RAW SALMON WITH LIME
LAMB CUTLETS IN FILO PASTRY
BANANA, KIWI AND APPLE SALAD

Introduction

Raw fish, à la japonaise, is becoming deservedly popular. It is nutritious, with a pleasing 'non-fishy' flavour. But it must be very fresh, bought and sliced on the day of serving.

The cutlets wrapped in pastry are very light – the pastry being the Greek filo. The salad is simple, exotic and pretty.

Cook's gear

A sharp long knife and pair of tweezers for the salmon.

A pastry brush for buttering pastry for the lamb.

A melon baller for the apples in the fruit salad – not necessary but effective.

Cook's tips

If the fishmonger cannot slice the salmon for you, lay the fillet skin side down on a board. Feel for the row of bones and extract them with pliers or tweezers.

Use a sharp long ham knife or carving knife to cut horizontal paper-thin slices.

Buy filo pastry from a Greek delicatessen. Keep the pastry covered with poly-wrap or a damp teatowel while working or while it is waiting to go in the oven, to prevent drying out.

To obtain double cutlets: ask the butcher to 'chine' the best end of lamb and to remove every *other* bone so that when the meat is sliced into cutlets each piece will have the meat of two cutlets but only one cutlet bone. Trim off all the fat, and leave the bones not longer than 5cm/2in. Or use tender lamb 'steaks' rather than cutlets.

In the fruit salad the acidity of lemon juice will help to prevent the banana and apple browning. Chilling helps too. Do not slice the

11

kiwi fruit too thinly or too far in advance — it might lost its firm texture.

Getting ahead
The salmon should be bought and prepared on the day of serving, but can be dished, covered with poly-wrap and refrigerated several hours in advance.

The cutlet parcels can be prepared up to 24 hours in advance but must be baked while the first course is eaten.

The fruit salad can be made three hours ahead and chilled.

Vegetable or salad?
Forget potatoes unless you really want them. The pastry will provide a little starch. Shredded courgettes are good: grate coarsely in advance (skin and all), salt lightly and leave to drain.

Squeeze out and toss in butter in a large pan for 35 seconds only, then serve promptly.

Japanese Raw Salmon with Lime

750g 1½lb very fresh raw
   salmon, cut as for smoked
   salmon
5 fresh limes

light olive oil
freshly ground black pepper
rock or sea salt

To serve
brown bread and butter

1　Cover each plate with the finely sliced salmon, without overlapping the slices.
2　Cut four limes in half. Put one half on each plate.
3　Using the finest gauge, grate outer rind (no pith) of remaining lime into a bowl. Squeeze juice into bowl.
4　Add the olive oil.
5　Just before serving, grind black pepper over salmon, sprinkle lightly with salt and spoon a little oil and lime dressing all over the fish.
6　Serve with brown bread and butter.

Lamb Cutlets in Filo Pastry

8 double lamb cutlets
50g 2oz butter
2 small onions, finely chopped
bunch fresh mint, finely
   chopped

salt, pepper and nutmeg
8 leaves filo pastry
melted butter

1 Remove all fat from lamb cutlets and season them with pepper.
2 Use a piece of trimmed lamb fat to grease a very hot, heavy frying pan. Brown the cutlets fast to sear both sides without cooking the meat inside. Remove from pan.
3 Heat butter in pan and slowly cook onion until soft.
4 Add mint. Cook for further minute. Season with salt, pepper and nutmeg. Allow to cool.
5 Set oven to 220°C/425°F/Mark 8.
6 Lay out filo leaves and brush with melted butter. Place a cutlet on each leaf.
7 Spoon onion mixture onto lamb.
8 Wrap with filo to make a parcel. Brush with more butter.
9 Bake for 10 minutes.

Banana, Kiwi and Apple Salad

4 red apples
5 kiwi fruit
3 bananas

4tbsp caster sugar
3tbsp Amaretto or rum

1 Using a melon baller shape the unskinned apple into balls.
2 Peel kiwi. Slice.
3 Peel bananas. Cut into chunks.
4 Put fruit together in bowl. Sprinkle over sugar. Pour over liqueur.
5 Chill. Before serving gently toss fruit to redistribute the alcohol.

MENU 3

OMELETTE SALAD
PAPRIKA CHICKEN
DANISH APPLE CAKE

Introduction
For some reason the British are prejudiced about cold eggs, other than hard-boiled. But this Danish first course of strips of cold omelette is very good. The paprika chicken is not too spicy, but has a rich red sauce, and the apple cake is tart, filling and good hot or cold. The trick, I am afraid, is a lot of whipped cream. Custard is good too, but after the eggs in the starter, more eggs should perhaps be avoided.

Cook's gear
Omelette or non-stick pan for the eggs.

Cook's tips
Make the omelettes with unseparated eggs, mixed rather than whisked, with a little water. They should be very thin and flat, not fluffy.

It is important that the wine goes into the chicken dish at the start so it can simmer for a good long time to lose its alcoholic harshness.

Dip the tomatoes into boiling water for five seconds to loosen their skins.

Sultanas are a good addition to the apple cake mixture.

Getting ahead
The omelette and dressing can be made the day before, but should be put together only at the last minute. The tomatoes can be peeled in advance, but slice them at the last minute.

The paprika chicken is excellent reheated, and can therefore be made a day, or even two, in advance, but add the soured cream at the last minute.

The apples and fried crumbs for the apple cake can both be cooked

14

the day before, but should not be put together until a few hours before serving, lest the crumbs become soggy.

Vegetable or salad?
Rice, noodles or mashed potato are essential for mopping up the sauce. One crisp green vegetable, such as spring cabbage, shredded finely and cooked fast and briefly, or perhaps slightly crisp fennel, would fit the bill.

Omelette Salad

3 two-egg omelettes, cold and cut in strips
3 tomatoes, peeled and seeded

3 anchovies, cut into small pieces
16 black olives

Dressing
3tbsp olive oil
1tbsp lemon juice

fresh or dried oregano or thyme
salt and pepper

1 Arrange strips of omelette in lattice pattern on a large flat serving dish, or on individual plates.
2 Fill in the gaps of the lattice with pieces of tomato, anchovy and olives.
3 Mix dressing ingredients together and spoon over the salad.

Paprika Chicken

2 chickens
50g 2oz flour seasoned with salt and pepper
3tbsp oil
100g 4oz butter
2 large onions, finely sliced
300ml ½pt white wine

2 cloves garlic, crushed
1tbsp paprika
4tbsp tomato purée
600ml 1pt chicken stock
2tbsp parsley, finely chopped
thyme
300ml ½pt soured cream

1 Joint chickens into eight pieces each.
2 Coat pieces with seasoned flour.
3 Heat oil and add butter. When melted and hot, brown chicken portions all over. Put to one side.
4 Fry onions until soft, adding more butter if necessary.

5 Add wine. Boil hard for 5 minutes.
6 Mix garlic, paprika, any remaining seasoned flour and tomato purée to smooth paste. Stir into pan.
7 Add stock. Bring to boil, stirring.
8 Return chicken to pan. Add parsley, thyme, salt and pepper. Barely simmer for 40 minutes or until chicken is tender.
9 Lift chicken onto serving dish. Spoon over sauce and swirl soured cream on top.

Danish Apple Cake

1.5kg 3lb tart eating apples	175g 6oz butter
butter	1tsp cinnamon
350g 12oz brown sugar	icing sugar
4 cups fresh coarse breadcrumbs	flaked browned almonds

To serve
half-whipped cream

1 Gently stew peeled and sliced apples until soft but not broken with a tablespoon of butter and 300g/10oz of sugar. Taste and add more sugar if necessary. Allow to cool.
2 Shape apple into a cake on a serving plate.
3 Slowly fry crumbs in butter, stirring continuously. Once butter has been absorbed crumbs start to brown and crispen fast – cool the base of the pan in cold water to stop the cooking. Add cinnamon and remaining brown sugar.
4 When cold, spoon crumbs over apple. Chill. Dust with icing sugar and sprinkle with flaked almonds. Serve with plenty of half-whipped cream.

MENU 4

PASTA ALLA CARBONARA
TURBOT AND SEAFOOD KEBABS
ORANGE YOGHURT SORBET

Introduction

The pasta is pretty, delicious, fattening and filling, so serve small portions, in old fashioned soup bowls with a rim if you have them. The kebab is plain and light, and will keep, dished up, quite happily in a warming drawer or cool oven. The yoghurt is not detectable in the sorbet but gives creaminess without adding richness.

Cook's gear

A spaghetti rake (wooden implement like a giant's hairbrush) is invaluable for fishing strands of pasta out of the water for testing, and for mixing and serving.

Kebab skewers for the turbot.

A sorbetière or ice cream maker is not essential, but the freezer must be efficient – the ice-making compartment of a refrigerator is no good.

Cook's tips

If cooking the pasta a little in advance (a good idea as the steam from boiling pasta gets the cook hot and bothered), butter it lightly to stop it sticking, but do not add the egg mixture until just before serving, or it will lose its creaminess.

If using an oven rotisserie with a kebab attachment, make sure the pieces of fish etc. are small enough for the eight of them to fit comfortably side by side. If using a grill, try to get wooden skewers (or use sharpened rosemary twigs, with the leaves removed). They are less murderously hot to hold. Warn guests about the heat of metal skewer handles.

To speed up freezing of the sorbet, have whisks and bowls well chilled before use.

If using a food processor for re-whisking, the mixture can be frozen

17

rock-solid and simply broken into chunks and processed to smooth creaminess. Refreeze.

Getting ahead

The pasta sauce can be prepared up to, but not including, the addition of the eggs and cream up to 48 hours in advance. Add the eggs and cream just before serving. The pasta can be cooked an hour or so before dinner and reheated in a little butter.

The kebabs will dry out if reheated, but can be kept warm for 15 minutes or so. Skewer them 12 hours in advance and brush with oil. Keep refrigerated.

Make sorbet anything from 6 hours to 5 days ahead. Remove from freezer half an hour before serving to soften slightly.

Vegetable or salad?

Rice is traditional with kebabs, but do not serve much – the first course is starchy. Do serve a green salad, either with or after the kebab – perhaps of iceberg lettuce and mint with an oil and vinegar dressing.

Pasta alla Carbonara

350g 12oz green tagliatelli	85g 3oz Pecorino or Gruyère
350g 12oz white tagliatelli	cheese, grated
1tbsp olive oil	85g 3oz butter, melted
175g 6oz lean ham, cut in	6 eggs
strips	4tbsp double cream
	salt and pepper

To serve
grated Parmesan cheese

1 Boil pasta in plenty of water. Drain and rinse with more hot water to remove surface starch.
2 Heat oil. Toss ham in it briefly then mix with the tagliatelli.
3 Mix remaining ingredients (except Parmesan) in a saucepan and stir over low heat until just beginning to thicken – do not allow to scramble.
4 Stir into pasta. Serve Parmesan separately.

Turbot Seafood Kebabs

500g 1lb turbot fillet, skinned	250g 8oz small open mushrooms
250g 8oz rindless streaky bacon rashers	melted butter
500g 1lb raw peeled scampi	sea salt and black pepper
500g 1lb small fresh scallops	4 lemons, halved

1 Cube turbot and wrap each piece in a strip of bacon.
2 Remove dark threadlike intestine from each scallop and the fibrous muscle from opposite orange 'coral'.
3 Thread a mixture of fish, seafood and mushrooms onto eight long skewers, pushing firmly together. Brush with melted butter.
4 Heat grill to maximum. Grill kebabs, turning once, until bacon is sizzling. Or bake at top of blazing oven; or grill on rotisserie for about 20 minutes.
5 Sprinkle with sea salt and pepper. Serve with juices from the grill tray and lemon halves.

Orange Yoghurt Sorbet

350ml 12fl oz concentrated frozen orange juice	300ml ½ pint plain yoghurt
1tsp gelatine powder	4tbsp icing sugar
	4 stiffly beaten egg whites

1 Allow orange juice to thaw to room temperature.
2 Put 8 tablespoons of water into a saucepan. Sprinkle over the gelatine. Leave for 10 minutes then heat very gently until runny and clear – do not allow to boil.
3 Pour into orange juice. Add yoghurt and sugar. Freeze until edges are solid but centre is still soft. Whisk until smooth. Return to freezer. Keep whisking at intervals until smooth and creamy.
4 Fold in egg whites. Refreeze.

MENU 5

ICED BORSCHT WITH CUMIN
ROAST FILLET WITH BACON
CINNAMON CHEESECAKE

Introduction

Fillet of beef costs a lot of money, but no-one need – or ought – to get much, and it is a big treat for a special dinner. The borscht is an elegant creamy version of the Russian classic and the cheesecake is, I immodestly think, the best there is.

Cook's gear

A liquidizer for the soup.

For the cheesecake a 22cm/9in deep flan ring or loose-bottomed cake tin (a 'spring-form' cake pan with a clip that releases the sides is ideal).

Cook's tips

Borscht is good hot too. Do not boil or it may curdle.

Fillet should be left for 10–15 minutes before carving for juices and colour to spread through the meat.

Rare or blue roast beef does not produce enough meat glaze to make good gravy. But rare beef doesn't need any anyway – just carve the meat on a dish that will collect any juices and spoon a little of that over each portion.

For a change from cinnamon cover the top of the cheesecake with lemon curd or with fresh fruit like seedless grapes or raspberries.

Getting ahead

Make the soup the day before and keep chilled. Or make the base (without the milk, lemon or cream) and freeze. Add the omitted ingredients after thawing and whisking until smooth.

Get the fillet of beef trimmed and prepared with bacon, but roast just before dinner.

20

The cheesecake is best made on the morning of the dinner, but very good after 24 hours too.

Vegetable or salad?
Potatoes sliced and baked in a pie dish until very tender, with garlic, cream and butter (gratin dauphinois), can be made in advance and reheated. A selection of lightly cooked fresh vegetables would be nice too. If you have a microwave oven, they are better pre-cooked, cooled, laid in neat shallow rows on the serving dish, covered in poly-wrap and reheated for a minute just before serving. They stay green and crisp. In the absence of a microwave, do one easy vegetable (say beans) and bake a few half tomatoes with a little chopped onion while the fillet is in the oven.

Iced Borscht with Cumin

1 large onion, sliced
250g 8oz potatoes, diced
    small
30g 1oz butter
500g 1lb raw beetroots,
    washed
600ml 1pt water
1 chicken stock cube
large bunch parsley
salt and pepper
pinch cumin
pinch ground cloves

pinch sugar
pinch grated nutmeg
600ml 1pt milk
300ml ½pt cream
lemon juice
150ml ¼pt soured cream
chopped chives

1 Cook onions and potato in butter very slowly until soft, keeping the saucepan covered and shaking frequently (about 30 minutes).
2 Simmer beetroots in the pint of water with stock cube, parsley and seasonings until tender. Top up with water as necessary to keep them covered.
3 Peel beetroots and liquidize with cooking liquid and potato mixture.
4 Add milk and cream and enough lemon juice to give a slight sharpness to the soup. Chill.
5 Pour into individual chilled dishes. Top with soured cream and chopped chives.

Roast Fillet with Bacon

1.75kg 3½lb trimmed beef
  fillet, from thick end
2tbsp made English mustard
8 rindless streaky bacon
  rashers
3tbsp sweet port   } for medium or
300ml· ½pt beef stock } well done
salt and pepper   } beef only

To serve
bunch watercress, washed

1   Set oven to maximum.
2   Remove any gristle or membrane from fillet.
3   Spread mustard all over fillet.
4   Lay bacon rashers across the meat.
5   Roast for 15 minutes then turn oven down to 220°C/425°F/Mark
    7. Roast 40 minutes more for rare, 45 minutes for medium and 50
    minutes for well done beef.
6   Put beef on serving dish. Leave to rest for 10 minutes.
7   Skim any fat from pan. Add port, boil until reduced to one
    tablespoon. Then add stock, salt and pepper. Boil one minute.
    Serve in gravy boat.
8   Twist the stalks off the watercress and 'plant' the bunch at the side
    of the beef. Carve at table.

Cinnamon Cheesecake

Crust
20 digestive biscuits, crushed   175g 6oz butter, melted
100g 4oz caster sugar

Filling
300g 10oz best quality soft   1 egg yolk
  cream cheese   1tsp vanilla essence
300ml ½pt double cream   ½tsp ground cinnamon
2 whole eggs   1½tbsp sugar

Topping
300ml ½pt soured cream   ground cinnamon
2tsp caster sugar

1 Set oven to 190°C/375°F/Mark 5.
2 Mix crust ingredients.
3 Line deep wide flan ring with an even layer of mixture, pressing it
   firmly to base and sides.
4 Bake for 15 minutes.
5 Mix filling ingredients until smooth. Pour into crust. Bake until
   filling sets (about 20 minutes).
6 When cool, carefully lift off flan ring and slide cake onto plate.
   Mix soured cream with caster sugar, spread over cake.
7 Dust top heavily with cinnamon.

MENU 6

FOUL MEDAMES
SWEDISH LAMB WITH DILL
BAKED APPLES IN ORANGE AND
HONEY SAUCE

Introduction

The wonderfully unattractive name, foul medames, denotes a very good dried bean, delicious served in the Middle Eastern way with garlic and olive oil as a starter. The lamb is Sweden's contribution to gastronomy – it really is very elegant and subtle, and the baked apples are homely and English. An odd mixture, but good.

Cook's gear

A pressure cooker would cut cooking time of beans, and a garlic press would be useful, but neither are essential.

A mincer if doing minced potatoes (see below).

A peeler and corer for the apples.

Cook's tips

Serve foul medames with hot pitta bread, cut into sticks, or fingers of hot toast. You use the bread to push the beans onto the fork and then to mop up the juices.

In the absence of fresh dill for the lamb, use dill seed, but strain it out of the sauce before serving; the sauce should be creamy and smooth.

Choose smallish apples for the dessert – no one can manage a great Bramley after two courses.

Cider can replace all or half the orange juice if preferred.

Getting ahead

The beans can be cooked and dressed a day ahead, but the tomatoes should be added just before serving.

The lamb can be successfully cooked a few days in advance, but the final addition of yolks and cream must be made only when reheating for serving.

24

The apples can be prepared in advance but baked just before dinner, not too much ahead of time – they will take 40 minutes to cook and are nicest served tepid rather than blazing hot, so put them in just before the guests are due to arrive.

Vegetable or salad?

The nicest potatoes to have with this dish are minced rather than mashed. Boil floury potatoes in their skins. Skin them and put them, while hot, through a mincer or ricer, allowing them to drop straight into the serving dish, looking like spaghetti. If doing this in advance, reheat in the serving dish, the top sprinkled with melted butter. Spinach (briefly boiled, squeezed dry, roughly chopped, and served with butter, pepper, salt and nutmeg) goes well with lamb.

Foul Medames

500g 1lb dried foul beans, soaked overnight	4tbsp spring onions, chopped
6tbsp olive oil	4tbsp parsley, chopped
sea salt and black pepper	4tbsp lemon juice
2 cloves garlic, crushed	few segments raw tomato for decoration

1   Simmer beans in unsalted water for 1–2 hours or until soft. (Pressure cooking takes about 30 minutes.) Drain.
2   Add oil, salt and pepper.
3   Stir in remaining ingredients, except tomatoes.
4   Tip into serving dish. Decorate with tomatoes. Serve just warm or cold.

Swedish Lamb with Dill

1.5kg 3lb lean lamb, cubed	850ml 1½pt chicken stock
1 onion, roughly sliced	50g 2oz butter
1 carrot, roughly chopped	30g 1oz flour
2tbsp chopped dill leaves or dill seeds	1tbsp lemon juice
1 bay leaf	3 egg yolks
salt and pepper	150ml ¼pt cream

1   Simmer lamb in tightly covered saucepan with vegetables, herbs, seasonings and stock for approximately one hour.

2 When tender, lift meat onto serving dish and keep warm.
3 Strain and skim liquid. If necessary make up quantity to 600ml/1pt with water.
4 Melt butter. Add flour. Cook for 30 seconds.
5 Add stock. Bring to boil, whisking. Boil fast for five minutes.
6 Add lemon juice. Check seasoning.
7 Mix yolks with cream. Add ladleful of hot sauce, stir well. Return to pan. Reheat without boiling. Pour over lamb.

Baked Apples in Orange and Honey Sauce

8 cooking apples
50g 2oz melted butter
6tbsp dried white breadcrumbs

2tbsp sultanas
finely grated rind and juice of 3 large oranges
4tbsp honey

To serve
double cream, whipped

1 Set oven to 190°C/375°F/Mark 5.
2 Core apples. Peel top half of each apple.
3 Brush each one with butter and roll in breadcrumbs.
4 Stand apples in ovenproof dish. Fill centre hole with sultanas and orange rind.
5 Spoon honey over top of apples and pour orange juice into dish.
6 Bake for 40–50 minutes or until soft and browned, basting with the juice occasionally.
7 Serve hot with thick cream.

MENU 7

GRILLED PRAWNS
VEAL BLANQUETTE WITH
BROAD BEANS AND CARROTS
PRUNE SORBET

Introduction

Prawns make a glamorous starter, but they should be bought raw –
live or frozen – if they are to be grilled. (If buying fresh boiled prawns
in their shells, either the pink ones or the tiny brown shrimps, they are
best served cold with hot bread and butter and lemon wedges.) The
blanquette can be made with English pie veal rather than the expensive
Dutch veal. The prune sorbet is oddly good – subtle and unusual.

Cook's gear

A sorbetière or ice cream maker is not essential, but the freezer must be
efficient – the ice-making compartment of a refrigerator is no good.

Cook's tips

If you are lucky enough to get live langoustines or Dublin Bay prawns
you will need courage to kill them: hold the head end still with a cloth,
grasp the tail with finger and thumb, and giving a twist and a yank, pull
off the tail fin, which will draw the intestinal tract with it. This cleans
the animal and kills it instantly. Then split the tail lengthwise up to the
thorax. The two halves will curl attractively when grilled.

A spoonful of plum brandy (slivovitz) or liqueur (mirabelle) in the
sorbet mixture will lift it into the grand-luxe class.

To speed up freezing of ice creams and sorbets, have all whisks,
bowls etc. well chilled before use.

If using a food processor for re-whisking, the mixture can be frozen
rock-solid and simply broken into chunks and processed to smooth
creaminess. Refreeze.

Getting ahead

The prawns can be ready on the grill, brushed with butter and lemon, but they must be grilled at the last minute.

The blanquette can be made up to 48 hours in advance, but the cream and egg yolks and the freshly boiled beans and carrots should only go in on re-heating.

The sorbet is best made not more than a week ahead – it can lose its smoothness if kept frozen too long.

Vegetable or salad?

The beans and carrots in the blanquette are adequate, but do provide rice or noodles to mop up the sauce.

Grilled Prawns

2kg 4lb large raw prawns	3tbsp fresh herbs, chopped
50g 2oz melted butter	salt and pepper
4 large lemons	

1 Lay large prawns on grill tray. (See note in Cook's tips.) If they are fairly small, thread them onto eight skewers. Brush with melted butter.
2 Cut two of the lemons into quarters. Squeeze the juice from the other lemons.

3 Heat grill to maximum. Grill prawns, turning once. Do not over-cook them. As soon as they are firm, transfer to heated serving dish.
4 Add lemon juice, herbs, salt and pepper to butter in grill pan. Pour over prawns. Serve with lemon quarters.

Veal Blanquette with Broad Beans and Carrots

1.5kg 3lb pie veal, cubed
3 small onions, sliced
half a lemon
bouquet garni; parsley stalks, bay leaf, blade of mace, stick of celery tied together
2tsp cornflour
salt and pepper

4 egg yolks
300ml ½pt double cream
500g 1lb baby carrots, just cooked
500g 1lb broad beans, just cooked
chopped parsley

1 Put veal in saucepan with onions, lemon and bouquet garni. Cover with cold water. Slowly bring to the boil and just simmer for 60 minutes, skimming scum off the surface every 10 minutes or so.
2 When veal is really tender, remove veal and onions to ovenproof serving dish – keep warm.
3 Discard bouquet garni. Mix cornflour with tablespoon of water and then add some of the hot stock. Mix well, then stir paste into remaining stock. Bring to boil, stirring. If sauce is still too thin, continue boiling to reduce and thicken. Season with salt and pepper.
4 Mix egg yolks with cream. Add tablespoon of hot sauce, mix well and return to pan. Do not allow sauce to boil at this stage but reheat very gently. Add carrots and beans to sauce and heat through. Pour over meat and onions and scatter parsley on top.

Prune Sorbet

350g 12oz dried prunes
600ml 1pt water
175g 6oz sugar

juice of 2 lemons
juice of 2 oranges
4 egg whites

1 Soak prunes overnight in the water.
2 Next day, add sugar and boil gently for five minutes. Allow to cool.

3 Remove stones from prunes. Liquidize prunes with cooking syrup, lemon and orange juice. Pass through a fine sieve to remove bits of skin.

4 Freeze until edges are solid but centre is still soft. Whisk until smooth. Return to freezer. Keep whisking at intervals until smooth and creamy.

5 Beat egg whites until stiff. Fold into sorbet. Freeze until solid. If mixture is too hard to scoop, remove to refrigerator for half an hour before serving.

MENU 8

TARAMASALATA
RIESLING CHICKEN
RED FRUIT SALAD WITH
BOODLES FOOL

Introduction
It is important to get a really flowery wine for the sauce, a sweetish Sylvaner or Riesling. Serve the taramasalata in tiny individual rame-kins if you have them – it is very rich. The diners, who do not know there is a creamy fool to follow, will have too much of it if it is left in a great bowl in the middle of the table.

Cook's gear
Processor or blender for the taramasalata.
   Cherry stoner for the red fruit salad.

Cook's tips
If the taramasalata curdles instead of forming a smooth emulsion, do not despair. Put another slice of crumbled bread into the empty machine, add a little water or lemon juice and process to a thick paste. Then add the curdled mixture a teaspoon at a time until it is light and smooth again. The more oil you add the blander and creamier will be the paste.
   For a really elegant look to the main dish, buy eight fresh chicken breasts instead of two whole chickens.
   Dip grapes into boiling water for a few seconds if they will not peel easily.

Getting ahead
The taramasalata keeps well in a cool place for a week or so, but do not have the fridge too cold or it may separate on warming to room temperature again.
   The chicken dish can be cooked the day before, but add the cream and yolks only when re-heating.

The red fruit salad should be made a few hours in advance to allow time for the juices to flow, but not more than 10 hours in advance, or it may look tired.

Vegetable or salad?
Small new potatoes cooked in their skins with mint would be excellent, with perhaps buttered leaf spinach. Or simply serve potatoes and a plain cos salad with a slightly lemony dressing.

Taramasalata

1 thick slice fresh white bread, crustless	2 cloves garlic
250g 8oz skinned smoked cods' roe	freshly ground black pepper
	300ml ½pt oil
	juice of ½ lemon

To serve
hot pitta bread or unbuttered
   toast

1   Soak bread in water. Squeeze almost dry. Crumble into a liquidizer or food processor.
2   Add cods' roe, garlic and plenty of black pepper. Run the machine.
3   Add oil very gradually, as if making mayonnaise. It will become a pale, thick paste.
4   Check seasoning. Add lemon juice. Keep covered until serving to prevent skin forming.
5   Serve with hot pitta bread or toast.

Riesling Chicken

2 chickens	bunch parsley
50g 2oz butter	250g 8oz grapes, peeled, halved, seeded
4 shallots, chopped	2tbsp flour
450ml ¾pt flowery white wine, preferably Riesling	2tbsp cream
450ml ¾pt chicken stock	

1   Joint each chicken into eight pieces.
2   Melt butter in large sauté pan. Brown chicken pieces all over. Remove from pan.

3   Cook shallots slowly in same pan until soft. Return chicken to pan.
4   Add wine, stock and parsley. Cover, bring to the boil and simmer until chicken is tender (about 40 minutes).
5   Lift out and arrange on hot serving dish. Scatter grapes over top. Keep covered.
6   Skim fat off stock. Boil rapidly until reduced to 450ml/¾pt. Mix two tablespoons of the fat with the flour then stir it back into the hot stock until boiling point is reached again. Check seasoning. Simmer for five minutes. Add cream and pour over chicken.

Red Fruit Salad and Boodles Fool

1kg   2lb assorted fresh red fruit (cherries, strawberries, redcurrants etc.)
4tbsp kirsch

2 small oranges
300ml ½pt double cream
3tbsp icing sugar

1   Prepare the red fruit as necessary, leaving small berries whole or in small clusters and cutting larger fruit into attractive and manageable pieces. Sprinkle with kirsch and chill.
2   Thinly pare rind off one orange. Cut the rind into the finest needleshreds (2cm/1in long). Put these in boiling water for five minutes, rinse under cold water and drain. Dry on absorbent paper.
3   Finely grate rind of remaining orange and squeeze the juice from both oranges.
4   Whip cream until stiff then slowly beat in the orange juice, grated rind and sugar.
5   Arrange the fruits in little groups and clusters on dinner-plates, leaving a gap in which to put a spoonful of the fool. Scatter the needleshreds on top of the fool.

MENU 9

JELLIED CONSOMMÉ WITH MOCK CAVIARE
BAKED GREY MULLET WITH HERBS
ALMOND CUPS WITH ICE CREAM

Introduction
The starter for this menu is one of those cooks 'cheats' that is ludicrously easy. It is delicious too. On the other hand, the biscuit cups for the ice cream are tricky and time-consuming. The grey mullet is simplicity itself.

Cook's gear
8 soup cups or bowls.

Something (teacups, ovenproof tumblers or metal moulds) to shape the pastry for the biscuits in the oven.

A sorbetière or ice cream maker is not essential, but the freezer must be efficient – the ice-making compartment of a refrigerator is no good.

Cook's tips
The consommé starter is rather good with lump-fish roe (mock caviare) spooned on top with a squeeze of lemon.

Check consommé label; some tinned consommé will not set – add ½oz of gelatine to each pint of liquid.

Any firm white fish (monkfish, haddock, halibut, sea bass) could be substituted for the mullet.

If there is no time for making biscuit cups and ice cream, buy commercial brandy-snaps, which are very good, and serve them with the best bought vanilla ice cream. Do the apricot sauce though – it makes all the difference.

If the biscuit cups are not dry though, they will lose their shape and crispness in a tin. If this happens re-bake briefly over the upside-down cups, and cool before filling.

To speed up freezing of ice creams and sorbets, have all whisks, bowls etc. well chilled before use.

34

If using a food processor for re-whisking, the mixture can be frozen rock-solid and simply broken into chunks and processed to smooth creaminess. Refreeze.

Getting ahead
Make the soup the day before.

Season and wrap the fish in foil up to 4 hours before dinner, but keep refrigerated – freshness is all-important with grey mullet.

Make the cups for the ice cream in advance. Store in an airtight container. Make the ice cream too and use an ice cream scoop to pre-ball it to save dishing up time at the last minute. Make the sauce the day before. It will need reheating however, so do not overboil it the first time.

Vegetable or salad
Very thinly sliced potatoes baked in layers with butter and thin slices of onion, go very well with the fish.

Barely cooked, crisp and green french beans with a sprinkling of dill weed are delicious too. If timing is likely to be a problem, a salad would be just as good.

Jellied Consommé with Mock Caviare

350g 12oz full fat cream
cheese e.g. Philadelphia

2 cans jellied beef consommé
4oz lump-fish roe

1 Liquidize three quarters of the soup with the cream cheese.
2 Pour into small individual soup cups and chill to set.
3 Melt the remaining soup. Cool without allowing to re-set.
4 Pour a thin layer of soup into each cup. Chill until set.
5 Serve with a spoon of caviare on each serving.

Baked Grey Mullet with Herbs

2kg 4lb whole grey mullet,
   cleaned
fresh sprigs of tarragon and
   parsley
100g 4oz melted butter

finely grated rind and juice of 2
   lemons
salt and freshly ground black
   pepper
2tbsp dry white wine

1 Set oven to 200°C/400°F/Mark 6.
2 Lay fish on a large sheet of foil, on a baking tray or roasting tin.
3 Brush inside and out with butter, and add a squeeze of lemon juice.
   Sprinkle with wine. Season with salt and pepper. Put a few herb
   sprigs into the stomach opening of fish.
4 Wrap foil round fish to form a parcel. Bake 50 minutes or until the
   flesh will lift off bone easily.
5 Chop remaining herbs finely.
6 When fish is cooked, dish it whole on a warm platter.
7 Heat remaining butter, lemon rind and juice, liquid from the fish
   and chopped herbs together in a frying pan. Boil up, and pour
   sizzling, over the fish. Serve at once.

Almond Cups with Ice Cream

Biscuits
100g 4oz butter
100g 4oz caster sugar
4 drops almond essence
4 eggs

50g 2oz flour
50g 2oz ground almonds
vanilla ice cream (recipe below)
apricot sauce (recipe below)

1   Set oven to 190°C/375°F/Mark 5.
2   Melt butter with sugar. Remove from heat.
3   Add almond essence and when mixture is tepid or cooler, beat in the eggs.
4   Sift in flour and almonds.
5   Spoon a tablespoon of mixture onto a greased warm baking tray. Spread into circle the size of a saucer. If baking tray is large, do two, well apart.
6   Bake for five minutes, until just brown at the edges. Allow to cool for few seconds until pliable.
7   Using a fish slice lift the biscuits onto upside-down teacups. Carefully mould to shape of teacup, and return biscuits – on cups – to oven. Bake until evenly browned (a few more minutes). Leave to cool on the cups. Make eight cups in all.
8   Just before serving, fill each pastry case with balls of vanilla ice cream, and serve with the hot apricot sauce.

Vanilla Ice Cream

850ml	1½pt	milk	10 egg yolks
450ml	¾pt	cream	vanilla essence
350g	12oz	caster sugar	

1   Set freezer to coldest temperature.
2   Slowly heat milk, cream and sugar to boiling point, stirring occasionally.
3   Pour boiling mixture from a height onto egg yolks mixed with four drops of vanilla essence. Whisk well while pouring.
4   Strain into roasting tin or ice trays. Cool. Freeze until just set (firmly set if using a processor).
5   Tip into a chilled bowl or processor. Whisk until smooth, pale and creamy. Refreeze.

Apricot Sauce

6tbsp	thick apricot jam	juice of half a lemon
200ml	⅓pt water	2tbsp brandy or rum

1   Stir everything together in a saucepan over low heat.
2   When jam has melted, boil to a syrupy consistency.
3   For a smooth texture, push through a sieve.

MENU 10

MUSHROOM AND CORIANDER PÂTÉ
LAMB WITH APRICOTS
AND ALMONDS
ICED PEAR SABAYON

Introduction

The taste of coriander goes oddly well with the concentrated mushroom flavour of the pâté. Serve with heated pitta bread cut in sticks, or hot toast fingers. The dessert is sophisticated and slightly complicated but really worth the effort.

Cook's gear

A liquidizer or processor for the pâté.

An electric hand whisk or a strong arm and stamina for the unelectrified to beat the sabayon.

A melon baller for extracting pear cores.

Cook's tips

To prevent guests being tempted to eat too much pâté which is extremely rich, serve it in tiny ramekins or in spoonfuls on small plates with a couple of crisp lettuce leaves.

The sabayon will not separate if it is thickened *slowly* over the heat — to give the eggs time to cook while being whisked. Then allow it to cool completely before folding in the whipped cream. The slightest hint of warmth makes the cream go runny.

Getting ahead

The pâté may be made up to three days ahead. Keep refrigerated.

The lamb may be made up to three days ahead. Keep refrigerated.

Poach the pears the day before. Make the sabayon on the morning of the party.

Vegetable or salad?

Rice is a must with the rather Middle-Eastern flavoured lamb.

38

Simmer long-grained rice in chicken stock – it makes an enormous difference to the flavour. Serve a salad to follow; perhaps a Greek one of finely shredded lettuce, peeled and shredded tomatoes, finely chopped unskinned cucumber, all tossed in olive oil with a little cumin, lemon juice, salt, pepper and crushed garlic.

Mushroom and Coriander Pâté

500g 1lb mushrooms	2tsp coriander berries, crushed
175g 6oz butter	150ml ¼pt soured cream
1 clove garlic, crushed	salt and freshly ground black pepper

1 Slice the mushrooms and fry in half the butter with garlic and coriander until they are well cooked. Allow to cool.
2 Liquidize with the pan juices. Beat in the remaining butter.
3 Add soured cream and season with salt and pepper. Chill before serving with fingers of toast or hot wholemeal rolls.

Lamb with Apricots and Almonds

250g 8oz dried apricots	2tsp brown sugar
1 stock cube	salt and pepper
2kg 4lb lean lamb, in large chunks	1tbsp flour worked together with 1tbsp butter
2tbsp oil	2tbsp slivered almonds
1 medium onion, chopped	

1 Set oven to 150°C/300°F/Mark 2.
2 Soak apricots with stock cube in a little boiling water.
3 Brown lamb chunks on all sides in hot oil. Fry onions gently until soft but not brown.
4 Put lamb in casserole. Add onions, apricots and their liquid and the sugar. Add water to come half way up casserole.
5 Season with salt and pepper if necessary.
6 Cover and cook for 3 hours or until very tender. Lift lamb and apricots onto serving dish.
7 Skim fat from liquid.
8 Whisk flour and butter mixture into the liquid while bringing to the boil. Simmer for a minute.
9 Check seasoning. Add nuts. Pour over meat.

Iced Pear Sabayon

300g 10oz sugar
600ml 1pt water
juice of 2 lemons
8 small ripe pears
5 egg yolks

2tbsp pear brandy (Eau de vie de Poire William)
300ml ½pt double cream
8 top sprigs of young mint

1 Put sugar, water and lemon juice into a saucepan and bring to boil, stirring occasionally.
2 Peel pears without removing stalks. Use a melon baller or teaspoon to remove the core from the underside as neatly as possible.
3 Boil the pears in the syrup until tender and glassy (anything from 12–40 minutes depending on ripeness). Ensure the syrup bubbles over them continuously to prevent discoloration.
4 Remove pears, drain well and set aside to cool. Then chill.
5 To make the sauce, reduce the syrup by rapid boiling to 300ml/ ½ pint.
6 Put syrup (slightly cooled), yolks and brandy into a bowl that will fit snugly over a saucepan of simmering water without the base of the bowl touching the water.
7 Whisk steadily and slowly over gentle heat until the mixture is thick and mousse-like and will leave a 'ribbon trail' when the whisk is lifted. Do not hurry the process, the mixture must end up warm, pale and thick as half-whipped cream, rather than just frothy.
8 Remove from heat and whisk occasionally until stone cold – stand bowl in cold water to speed up the process – then chill.
9 Whip the cream until thick but still just runny. Fold into the egg mixture. Chill.
10 Put each chilled pear on a board, and slice through it, from rounded end towards the stem, without quite severing the slices from the stalk end. Fan slices out slightly.
11 Pour the sauce on chilled dessert plates to cover the base generously. Carefully lay a pear on each, and add a sprig of mint.

MENU 11

PUMPKIN AND TARRAGON SOUP
SAUTÉ OF LAMB WITH PEAS
FRESH FRUIT FLAN

Introduction

Few Englishmen profess to like pumpkin, but I have not met anyone who did not like this soup. The sweetness of the pumpkin is cut by the lemon and tarragon, and the texture is satin smooth. The flan is spectacular to look at but requires a bit of skill to do. A couple of perfect figs or a single peach for each guest could replace it for the hard-pressed cook.

Cook's gear

A liquidizer for the soup.
  A flameproof serving dish for the lamb.
  A paint or pastry brush to put the jam glaze on the flan.

Cook's tips

Pumpkin in tins will do fine if fresh pumpkin is not available. Dried tarragon is not bad either, but you need a lot of it – it seems to lose flavour when dried.

An English butcher will probably express horror at the extravagance of using the eye of the meat only, but the trimmings are used too, tell him.

In timing the lamb, the trick is not to keep it hot for long or it will lose its tenderness and pinkness. Let it cool and re-heat rapidly in the hot sauce with the peas.

Few people get the apricot glaze on the flan right the first time – the trick is to have it almost cold, so rather thick, when painting it on. It should cover the fruit in a deep shine. Do not be concerned that the flan will be too sweet – the fruit is raw and unsweetened, and could do with the jam.

Getting ahead

Make the soup up to two days in advance. Keep refrigerated.

The lamb can be prepared and marinated in the olive oil 24 hours in advance, and the sauce can be made the day before. But the cooking must be done not more than 30 minutes before dinner.

Make pastry case a few days in advance and store in a tin. If it goes soft, rebake briefly on day of eating. Assemble flan not more than four hours before dinner.

Vegetable or Salad?

Vegetables are unnecessary as the main dish contains peas, but mashed potatoes, re-heated with butter in the oven, would be delicious.

Pumpkin and Tarragon Soup

500g 1lb pumpkin
1 large onion, sliced
50g 2oz butter
500g 1lb potatoes, peeled and sliced
1 small clove garlic
600ml 1pt good chicken stock

salt and pepper
4 sprigs tarragon, just the leaves
600ml 1pt creamy milk
squeeze of lemon juice
3tbsp cream

1 Peel pumpkin, discarding seeds. Cut into chunks.
2 Slowly cook onion in butter until soft and transparent.
3 Add pumpkin, potato and garlic. Cover pan. Cook until vegetables are soft (15–20 minutes).
4 Add stock, salt and pepper and half the tarragon leaves. Bring to the boil.
5 Liquidize. Add milk. Reheat without boiling.
6 Add remaining tarragon. Flavour with lemon juice.
7 Stir in cream. Serve hot or chilled.

Sauté of Lamb with Peas

4 racks or best ends of lamb
2tbsp olive oil
1 bay leaf
1 slice onion

1 clove garlic, crushed
pepper
butter for frying

For the sauce

bones and trimmings from lamb	1tbsp butter
3 shallots	1tbsp flour
1 stock cube	salt and pepper
2tbsp tomato purée	500g 1lb fresh/frozen tiny young peas
1tbsp port	

1   Trim all fat, skin and bone from the meat to leave four cylinders of lamb, consisting of the prime 'eye' of the meat only. Slice across into bite sized chunks. Keep the bones and trimmings for the sauce. Discard any fat.
2   Put the lamb pieces into a bowl with the oil, crumbled bayleaf, onion, garlic and ground pepper – no salt.
3   Chop bones and put them into a saucepan with the meat trimmings, shallots, stock cube, tomato purée, port and enough water to cover them. Put on a lid and simmer gently for one hour.
4   Strain stock and lift off any fat. Melt butter in a clean pan and stir in the flour. Add the stock and whisk until boiling. Boil rapidly until the sauce is of a thin syrupy consistency. Check seasoning.
5   To cook the lamb, heat a tablespoon of butter in a large heavy frying or sauté pan. Fry the lamb as fast as possible until evenly brown all over but still pink inside. Cook only a few pieces at a time and put them into a flameproof dish as they are done.
6   Tip off any fat from the pan and add the sauce, stirring in any sediment stuck on the bottom.
7   Add the peas to the lamb, pour over the sauce and boil briefly to cook the peas and re-heat the lamb.

Fresh Fruit Flan

250g 8oz plain flour	2 egg yolks
pinch of salt	1tsp vanilla essence
85g 3oz ground almonds	175g 6oz butter, softened
85g 3oz caster sugar	

For the top

750g 1½lb selection of fruits: grapes, oranges, apples, strawberries, etc.	4tbsp apricot jam
	squeeze of lemon juice
	1tbsp water

To serve
whipped cream

1 To make pastry with a machine: assemble all ingredients and mix to a soft paste. Do not overwork the pastry.
2 To make pastry by hand: sift flour, salt and almonds onto a worktop or into a large bowl.
3 Make a space or well in the middle of the flour, and put in the remaining pastry ingredients.
4 With the fingers of one hand mix centre ingredients to a paste and then gradually incorporate the flour and almonds. Lightly knead into a smooth ball.
5 Chill pastry before use.
6 Set oven to 200°C/400°F/Mark 6.
7 Press or roll pastry into an oval or circle of about 1cm/½in thickness on a large baking tray.
8 Bake until golden in middle and browned at edges.
9 Allow to cool and harden on tray before moving to serving plate.
10 Melt apricot jam with lemon juice. Sieve. Cool. Lightly brush top of pastry with jam.
11 Cut fruit into neat uniform pieces. Arrange in rows along pastry, contrasting the colours of adjacent rows. Get as much fruit into each row as possible.
12 Glaze top of fruit with remaining jam. Serve with cream.

MENU 12

SMOKED HADDOCK SOUP
FILLET OF BEEF CARPACCIO
TARTE NORMANDE

Introduction
Sometimes a dinner with a hot starter and a cold main course is easier to manage than the usual cold-then-hot arrangement. This main course is not just cold, but raw, but do not be put off by that. It is a beautiful, light, very elegant dish and even people who like their steaks well done have been astonished to find themselves liking it. Don't try it on strangers, however.

Cook's gear
A liquidizer for the soup.

A meat mallet or rolling pin and tweezers for removing sinew from the beef.

Cook's tips
Kipper fillets or smoked cod give a similar soup, but smoked mackerel is too oily.

To skin tomatoes: dip them in boiling water for 5–8 seconds first.

When laying out the beef make sure the slices do not overlap – they lose their good colour if they do.

If slicing the beef fillet yourself, chill it until nearly, but not quite, frozen, then slice across against the grain. Other steak (flank, shin, skirt, rump or sirloin) will do too, but is not as butter-soft as fillet and has more sinews and fat to remove, and the slices, if cut properly against the grain, might be rather small.

Fresh cherries, plums, figs, pears or peaches may be used instead of the apples in the tarte. Treat pears as instructed for apples. Stone smaller fruit and scatter over the filling. Halve figs, arrange rounded side up.

Getting ahead

Make the soup the day before.

You can prepare the sauce for the beef up to two days and the beef one day ahead. Make sure the slices of beef do not overlap – store between layers of poly-wrap. Dish up on plates on the day of the dinner.

The tarte is best made on the day of eating. If made the day before, or if frozen after baking, warm slightly before serving.

Vegetable or salad?

Hot potatoes are unconventional but wonderfully good with, or after, raw beef – especially French fries. But if these are impractical settle for a salad of boiled potatoes dressed while hot with vinaigrette then allowed to cool to room temperature, and any green salad.

Smoked Haddock Soup

750g 1½lb smoked haddock fillet	850ml 1½pt fish or chicken stock
600ml 1pt milk	salt and pepper
30g 1oz butter	2 tomatoes, skinned
30g 1oz flour	1tbsp chopped parsley

1 Simmer haddock gently in the milk for eight minutes or until cooked.
2 Strain, keeping the liquid.
3 Cool. Remove skin and bones.
4 Melt butter in saucepan. Stir in flour. Pour back the milk. Stir until boiling.
5 Add stock, haddock, salt and pepper to taste.
6 Liquidize. Reheat without boiling.
7 Quarter the tomatoes. Remove the seeds. Cut flesh into thin strips and toss in chopped parsley.
8 Just before serving add tomatoes to soup.

Fillet of Beef Carpaccio

1kg   2lb   fillet steak, cut across grain into very fine slices

Sauce

3tbsp yoghurt
3tbsp double cream
3tbsp mayonnaise
1tbsp made English mustard

salt and pepper
½tsp creamed horseradish
lemon juice

1   Flatten slices of beef between two sheets of poly-wrap, using a mallet or rolling pin. Carefully remove all sinews.
2   When slices are as thin as possible, spread over dinner plates without overlapping.
3   Mix together first four sauce ingredients.
4   Flavour to taste with the remaining ingredients.
5   Serve sauce separately.

Tarte Normande

Pastry

250g 8oz plain flour
175g 6oz butter
2 egg yolks

2tbsp iced water
pinch of salt

Almond cream

100g 4oz caster sugar
100g 4oz butter
1 egg, whole
1 egg yolk

50g 2oz plain flour
100g 4oz ground almonds
1tbsp cream

Fruit filling

5 small ripe eating apples
4tbsp smooth apricot jam

1tbsp lemon juice

1 Pastry: rub butter into flour.
2 Add yolks mixed with water and salt. Mix to a soft dough. Chill.
3 Roll out pastry to line 30cm/10in flan ring or dish. Prick with fork. Chill.
4 Set oven to 220°C/425°F/Mark 7.
5 Almond cream: beat sugar and butter together until pale.

6 Mix in eggs, flour, almonds and cream. Spread mixture in pastry case.
7 Peel apples. Halve from stalk down through core. Remove core, keeping apple-halves intact.
8 Slice nine half-apples into segments, keeping all the slices together.

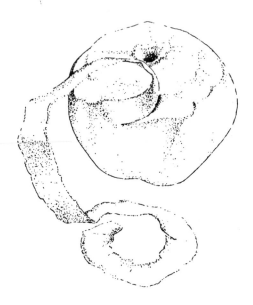

9 Arrange eight half-apples around the almond cream, rounded side up. Put ninth half in middle. Press firmly into cream.
10 Melt jam slowly with lemon juice. Cool until thickening, then use about half to coat apples.
11 Bake for 15 minutes. Turn oven down to 180°C/350°F/Mark 4. Bake for further 20 minutes.
12 Remove from oven when pastry is crisp, apples cooked and almond cream risen and brown.
13 Brush flan top with more jam. Return to oven for 10 minutes. Serve lukewarm.

MENU 13

FOUR BEAN SALAD
VEAL AND WILD RICE IN PASTRY
MINCEMEAT ICE CREAM

Introduction

The simple bean salad looks pretty served on individual plates. Hot bread handed separately is good. The veal needs nothing with it except perhaps a salad – and even that is not necessary, the guests having had their vitamins with the beans! The ice cream is a cheat, but a very good one.

Cook's gear

A large flat baking tray for the veal.

An ice cream scoop (optional).

Cook's tips

Substitute peas (mangetout, frozen garden peas, French tinned petits pois, cooked dried peas like chickpeas or black-eyed peas) for any of the beans if you cannot get what you want.

Pork fillet will do to replace the veal escalopes and is less expensive. Long grain brown rice can replace the wild rice if necessary.

Greek halva (sesame and nut confectionery bought at Greek or Jewish delicatessens) makes wonderful ice cream too. Substitute it for the fruit mincemeat. It is nicer in summer than mincemeat, which reminds one of Christmas.

Getting ahead

Prepare the beans on the morning of the dinner but do not add dressing or almonds until half an hour before eating.

Make filling for the veal the day before. Assemble a few hours in advance and bake just before dinner.

Make the ice cream a few days in advance, scoop into balls and return to freezer.

Vegetable or salad?
A simple green salad, served after or with the veal, would go well. Finely sliced fennel and iceberg lettuce, with a little mint in a vinaigrette dressing, would be perfect.

Four Bean Salad

small tin flageolet beans
small tin butter beans
250g 8oz frozen or fresh
   broad beans
250g 8oz fresh French beans
2tbsp flaked almonds
1tbsp olive oil

3tbsp salad oil
1tbsp red wine vinegar
1tbsp mixed chopped chives,
   parsley and mint
1 small clove garlic, crushed
salt and pepper

1   Rinse and drain canned beans.
2   Boil French beans and broad beans in salted water. When just tender rinse under cold water.
3   Fry almonds in oil until beginning to brown. Allow to cool.
4   Mix remaining ingredients in screw-top jar. Shake well. Pour over beans. Toss.
5   Put into clean serving dish. Scatter almonds over top just before serving.

Veal and Wild Rice in Pastry

8 small veal escalopes, beaten
   out thin
oil and butter for frying
4 rashers rindless streaky
   bacon, chopped
1 onion, chopped
250g 8oz button
   mushrooms, sliced

250g 8oz cooked wild rice or
   mixture of wild and brown
   rice
fresh or dried marjoram
salt and freshly ground black
   pepper
500g 1lb puff pastry
beaten egg

For the sauce
150ml ¼pt soured cream
grated rind and juice of 1 lemon

freshly chopped parsley

1 Set a large sieve over a bowl.
2 Fry veal escalopes on both sides in hot oil until barely brown. Cut into thin strips. Remove to sieve.
3 Fry first bacon, then onion, then mushrooms until softened. Tip into sieve with the veal, allowing juices to drain into the bowl. Stir rice into meat and vegetables. Season well with marjoram, salt and pepper. Allow to cool.
4 Set oven to 220°C/425°F/Mark 7.
5 Roll out three-quarters of the pastry very thinly to a rectangle of approximately 20cm × 30cm/8in × 12in. Place on a lip-less baking tray (or on the back of a lipped tray) and pile veal and rice mixture down the centre.
6 Fold pastry edges up to form sides to the pastry case, leaving centre open.
7 Cut strips from the left-over pastry and arrange them in a lattice pattern over the meat. Tuck them under the pastry base to secure. Brush with beaten egg.
8 Bake 20–25 minutes until pastry is cooked and browned.
9 Mix sauce ingredients with the drained frying juices and season with salt and pepper. Heat without boiling. Hand separately.

Mincemeat Ice Cream

850ml 1½pt best vanilla ice cream
500g 1lb mincemeat
2tbsp rum

1 Mix rum with mincemeat.
2 Thaw ice cream until just soft enough to beat in the mincemeat.
3 Refreeze.

MENU 14

CLAM CHOWDER
HONEY AND GINGER SPARE RIBS
CHESTNUT ROLL

Introduction
This is a good, unusual winter menu. The chowder is hefty, the ribs very light, and the chestnut roll positively wicked – deceptively mousse-like and light, but stacked with calories and cream.

Cook's gear
A rack or trivet to keep the ribs off the bottom of the roasting tin is a good idea though not essential.

The chestnut roll needs a good wide baking tray, and some grease-proof paper to line it. Also a teatowel to help with the rolling up.

Cook's tips
Of course, if fresh clams are easily had, and cheap, they can be used instead of the tinned ones. Buy them ready shucked, and cover them with water. Simmer until just tender, then use water and clams in the soup.

The trick with spare ribs is to get them really well cooked – the fat will keep them juicy, and they need to be well browned for crispness and flavour.

Do not worry if the chestnut cake falls to pieces on rolling up – it will taste wonderful anyway and last minute dusting with icing sugar will make it look fine.

Getting ahead
Make the clam chowder up to 48 hours ahead and refrigerate.

Marinate the spare ribs for between 4 and 48 hours, but roast immediately before serving.

Make the chestnut roll 12 to 24 hours in advance – it will roll up more easily. Roll and fill with cream up to 6 hours ahead of time.

52

Vegetable or salad?

Small baked potatoes, split, the flesh mixed with butter, grated cheese and lightly fried chopped spring onion, re-filled and reheated would be delicious. So would a sweetish salad – say chicory and apple in an oil and vinegar dressing.

Clam Chowder

100g 4oz smoked salt pork fat, finely diced	50g 2oz butter
	2tbsp flour
2 large Spanish onions, chopped	600ml 1pt milk
	1 400g 15oz tin of clams
500g 1lb new potatoes, peeled and diced	salt and black pepper
	5–6 tablespoons cream

1   Fry diced fat until it runs. Add onions. Fry until fat pieces are crisp and onions soft. Remove fat.
2   Add potatoes and butter. Cover and cook until potatoes are half done.
3   Stir in flour, then milk. Stir until boiling then add clams and their liquid. Season well and pour in cream. Reheat without boiling.

Honey and Ginger Spare Ribs

24 skinned belly of pork pieces (American spare ribs)

For the marinade

4tbsp runny honey	2tbsp tomato purée
4tbsp soy sauce	1 lemon, juice and rind
1 garlic clove, crushed	salt and pepper
1tbsp ground ginger	

1   Mix marinade ingredients together and pour over ribs. Leave five hours or longer.
2   Heat oven to 250°C/500°F/Mark 9.
3   Bake ribs on wire rack over a roasting tin until dark brown and sizzling, basting occasionally with the juices (20–30 minutes).

Chestnut Roll

6 eggs, separated
175g   6oz caster sugar
500g   1lb tin unsweetened
  chestnut purée

finely grated rind and juice of 2
  oranges
300ml   ½pt double cream,
  whipped
icing sugar

1   Set oven to 200°C/400°F/Mark 6.
2   Line a large roasting tin with foil. Brush lightly with oil and dust with flour.
3   Beat egg yolks with sugar until a thick, pale mousse. (If whisking the mousse with a hand whisk, put the bowl over a saucepan of simmering water to speed things up. Whisk until thick enough to leave a ribbon-like trail when the whisk is lifted.)
4   Beat purée with juice and rind of one orange until smooth. Stir into mousse.
5   Whisk egg whites until stiff. Stir one tablespoon of egg white into the chestnut mixture. Fold in the rest. (Do not overmix.)
6   Pour into roasting tin. Bake for 20 minutes or until risen, cooked and browned at the edges. Slide cake (and paper) onto wire cooling rack. Leave overnight.
7   Next day: whip cream, add grated rind and juice of remaining orange. Sweeten with icing sugar. Spread over cake and roll up like a Swiss roll, removing paper as you go.
8   Dust top with icing sugar.

MENU 15

LASAGNE RING MOULD
MIDDLE EASTERN SPINACH LAMB
STRAWBERRY PASTRIES

Introduction

The starter is a ring-shaped savoury custard, light, but rich. The lamb is a simple sauté of lamb and spinach, served with yoghurt. To avoid the temptation to tuck into too much rich pudding, the pastries should be small and neat and served on individual.plates.

Cook's gear

If possible, use a plain ring mould for the lasagne. A small cake tin or charlotte mould will do but as there will not be a hole in the middle of the custard, it will be less easy to serve neatly and will take 10 minutes or so longer to cook.

Cook's tips

Allow the lasagne custard to cool a little before turning out; it will be a little firmer if not too hot.

Two saucepans might be better than one for the lamb. You need plenty of room for tossing and turning.

To loosen tomato skins, dip them in boiling water for five seconds.

Serve the strawberry sauce poured round, not over, the pastries – it looks prettier. Add it only at the last minute to prevent the pastry becoming soggy.

Getting ahead

Bake the lasagne the day before or on the morning of the party. Reheat by standing the mould in a bowl or roasting tin of near-boiling water for 15 minutes or so before turning out to serve.

The lamb can be cooked ahead, but add the spinach only on reheating.

Bake the pastry a few days in advance – store in airtight container. Assemble 4–5 hours before dinner. Add sauce at the last minute.

Vegetable or Salad?

Instead of rice a starchy dried pulse like lentils or haricot beans would be good, but apart from that, there is no need for any green vegetable or salad – the dish contains spinach after all.

Lasagne Ring Mould

250g 8oz lasagne	2 whole eggs
4 rashers rindless, streaky bacon chopped	2 egg yolks
	300ml ½pt cream
butter for frying	300ml ½pt milk
1 large onion, finely chopped	salt and pepper
100g 4oz Cheddar cheese, grated	

1   Cook lasagne in boiling salted water for 15–20 minutes or until tender. Rinse under hot running water to remove surface starch.
2   Set oven to 190°C/375°F/Mark 5.
3   Line a buttered ring mould with a single layer of pasta.
4   Fry bacon in a teaspoon of butter until just brown. Add onion and cook until very soft, adding more butter if necessary.
5   Mix cheese, eggs, cream and milk. Add contents from frying pan. Check seasoning.
6   Carefully pour mixture into mould. Stand mould in roasting tin two-thirds full of hot water. Cover with foil.
7   Bake for 45 minutes or until custard has set. Cool 10 minutes.
8   Place heated serving dish upside down over mould. Invert mould and plate. Give a sharp shake to dislodge lasagne onto plate.

Middle Eastern Spinach Lamb

2tbsp oil	salt and pepper
1.5kg 3lb lean lamb, cut into chunks	750g 1½lb spinach, washed and dried
250g 8oz onions, chopped	

To serve

500g 1lb tomatoes, skinned, seeded and quartered	500g 1lb boiled rice
	300ml ½pt yoghurt

1   Heat oil in very large heavy saucepan. Add meat and onions. Cover and cook slowly for one hour, shaking the pan frequently to prevent scorching. Add salt and pepper.
2   Break spinach leaves into small pieces. Add to pan 10 minutes before end of cooking time, and keep stirring and turning until soft and bright green.
3   Tip the casserole and juices onto a bed of hot rice. Decorate with the tomato pieces and hand the yoghurt separately.

Strawberry Pastries

350g   12oz puff pastry (frozen is fine)
beaten egg
2tbsp best strawberry jam
750g   1½lb fresh strawberries

300ml   ½pt double cream, stiffly whipped
175g   6oz icing sugar

1   Roll the pastry into a rectangle measuring about 30cm/12in ×
21cm/9in. Cut across into three, and then lengthwise into six –
giving 18 small rectangles measuring 5cm/2in × 7cm/3in.
2   Wet a baking tray and lay the pieces on it. Prick them all over with
a fork, and brush lightly with beaten egg. Use the back of a knife or
the tines of a fork to mark a criss-cross pattern on the top of half
the rectangles. Leave to rest for half an hour in a cool place.
3   Bake in a hot oven (240°C/475°F/Mark 8) for 10 minutes or until
brown, then carefully turn each piece over to dry the other side;
when baked they should be crisp.
4   Choose the eight best unpatterned pieces. Spread carefully with
jam.
5   Slice half a pound of the strawberries and add them to the whipped
cream. Stir carefully. Put into the freezer for half an hour to
solidify further.
6   Spoon the mixture onto the pastry bases, as neatly as you can. Put
the eight best patterned pieces on top of the cream. Neaten up the
cream sides.
7   Liquidize the remaining strawberries with the icing sugar for the
sauce.

MENU 16

GUACAMOLE
CHICKEN BREASTS WITH
RICOTTA AND SPINACH
PEACH SHORTCAKE

Introduction
The combination of avocado and tomato is a generally popular starter. Chicken breasts can now be bought separately for elegantly shaped main course helpings. The pudding is an old fashioned, luxurious, fattening extravaganza.

Cook's gear
A processor makes light work of puréeing the ricotta and spinach and making the pastry; just whizz everything together briefly.

Use the processor or a coffee grinder to grind the hazelnuts.

Cook's tips
Avocado pears can be very stringy (with a tendency to discolour rapidly) at the beginning of the summer when we are getting southern late-season fruit. Buy one avocado and ask the greengrocer to open it up so that you can decide on the evidence whether to proceed. You want bright yellow smooth flesh with a green border near the skin – no grey spots near the stalk.

The guacamole mixture is good filled into hollowed-out skinned tomatoes, or red apples, or strips of cucumber with the seeds removed.

If you must use tinned peaches for the shortcake, try to get the white (Japanese or South African) variety.

Getting ahead
Do not do the starter too far ahead – about two hours at most. Keep covered closely and chilled, which helps prevent discoloration.

The chicken breasts can be prepared, even the day before, up to the point of baking, but should be cooked at the last minute; timing is important to get that just-cooked juiciness.

59

The pastry may be made a few days in advance and kept in an airtight container, and the cream can be whipped eight hours ahead. Assemble not more than two hours in advance of dinner.

Vegetable or salad?
The chicken dish is fairly austere, so perhaps a little luxury creamy or buttery mashed potatoes would be in order, or some long grain rice, first boiled then tossed in hot oil with a few shreds of bacon. Follow with a salad rather than any more vegetables – you have the spinach in the chicken.

Guacamole

4 large ripe avocado pears, mashed or chopped
1 small onion, minced or chopped
juice of 1 lemon
2tbsp olive oil
2 cloves garlic, crushed
2tbsp chopped fresh tomato
small pinch of coriander or 1tsp fresh coriander leaves, chopped
salt and pepper

1 Mix everything together, adding the avocado last.
2 Spoon into serving dish. Chill.
3 Serve with hot toast.

Chicken Breasts with Ricotta and Spinach

250g 8oz spinach leaves, stalks removed
250g 8oz ricotta, cream cheese or sieved curd cheese
salt and pepper
1 clove garlic, crushed
8 chicken breasts, skinned and boned
melted butter

1 Cook the spinach for 2–3 minutes in boiling water, keeping the leaves as whole as possible.
2 Set aside eight whole leaves. Squeeze all the liquid out of the remainder, and purée with the cheese, salt, pepper and garlic.
3 Set oven to 220°C/425°F/Mark 7.
4 Make a horizontal slit in each breast to create a pocket. Fill with the spinach and cheese mixture.
5 Wrap each chicken breast in a whole spinach leaf. Brush with melted butter and bake, covered, for 25 minutes.

Peach Shortcake

175g 6oz hazelnuts
250g 8oz butter
175g 6oz caster sugar
300g 10oz flour
pinch of salt

600ml 1pt double cream,
    stiffly whipped
8 fresh peaches
icing sugar

1 Brown hazelnuts in a hot oven. Take them out and rub them in a clean teatowel to remove the skins. Grind the nuts in a processor or coffee grinder. Take care not to over-grind them or they will become oily.
2 Beat butter with sugar until pale and fluffy.
3 Sift flour and salt into mixture. Add nuts. Fold together carefully. Chill for 30 minutes.
4 Set oven to 190°C/375°F/Mark 5.
5 Divide pastry into three equal portions. Press or roll each portion into a flat round the size of a dinner plate. Slide onto baking trays and bake for 12 minutes or until brown at the edges.
6 Allow to cool slightly before removing to wire rack. They will crispen as they cool. While still warm cut one of the pastry circles into eight segments.
7 Skin and slice peaches. Fold into cream. Sandwich two pastry rounds together with half the mixture. Spread remaining mixture on top. Set the pastry segments into the cream, each one at a slight angle. Dust with icing sugar.

MENU 17

GRILLED GOAT'S CHEESE SALAD
DUCK WITH BLACKCURRANTS AND PORT
PETITS POTS AU CAFÉ

Introduction

The grilled cheese is surprisingly good and very pretty to look at. It must be arranged on individual plates, however – it looks a mess on one big dish. The duck with blackcurrants is expensive, but worth it, and the little pots of custard – and they should be very little ones – are a smooth rich treat to end with.

Cook's gear

Use coffee cups or tiny ramekins if you do not have the traditional *petits pots*.

Plain white plates show the first course off best, if you have them.

Cook's tips

Buy fresh ducks if you can – it is impossible to tell the quality of a frozen duck. The backbone should be pliable when pressed, not rigid, and the feet should have smooth, not horny, scales. Two large ducks or four tiny ones would do instead of the three specified.

Tinned or frozen blackcurrants are fine, but halve the sugar if using ready-sweetened ones.

Two tablespoons of cassis liqueur can replace the port if preferred.

The coffee custards can be given an interesting grainy texture and 'real coffee' taste by the addition of a tablespoon of finely ground *fresh* coffee instead of the liquid coffee essence.

Getting ahead

Arrange the salads, except the apple balls and dressing, on the dishes on the morning of the party and cover each plate with poly-wrap. Refrigerate. Add the lemon-soaked apples and dressing an hour or so before serving.

The ducks can be roasted a few hours in advance and reheated, but they should not be done the day before, for fear of that 'reheated' taste. Do them in good time to make the sauce before going for a bath or to change.

The petits pots au café can be made the day before, but should be served at room temperature, not chilled, so take them out of the cold in good time.

Vegetable or salad?

Peas, with good reason, are a classic with duck. To avoid last-minute boiling you might bake them *à la française*: put them in a buttered dish with a sliced onion, sprig of mint, spoon of sugar, crushed clove of garlic, a shredded small lettuce, pepper and salt. Cover with buttered foil and bake under the ducks for an hour or so, depending on the age (or condition – frozen or fresh) of the peas. They should emerge soft, buttery and with most of the juice evaporated. If very wet boil off, rather than tip off, the liquid. They reheat perfectly.

Grilled Goat's Cheese Salad

8 thick slices from any fat cylindrical soft goat's cheese	3–4 red apples
	1tbsp lemon juice
1–2 red lettuces (radicchio)	85g 3oz walnut halves
2–3 heads Belgian chicory	

For the dressing

3tbsp salad oil	2tsp vinegar
1tbsp walnut oil	salt and black pepper

1 Lay the slices of cheese in the bottom of the grill tray.
2 Arrange radicchio and chicory leaves on eight plates, like the petals of a large flower – chicory and radicchio alternating.
3 Using a melon baller, scoop 30 or 40 balls out of the *unskinned* apples (or cut small dice). Toss them in the lemon juice and divide them between the salads. Leave a space in the middle of each plate for the cheese.
4 Dot the walnuts about, cover the plates and keep them in a cool place.
5 Shortly before dinner whisk together the dressing ingredients and sprinkle over the salads.
6 Just before serving, grill the cheese under blazing heat to brown the

top and warm through. Lift carefully onto the salads and serve at once.

Duck with Blackcurrants and Port

3 × 2kg/4lb ducks
salt
2 unpeeled cloves garlic
4tsp brown sugar or blackcurrant jam

100g 4oz blackcurrants
1 wineglass port
100g 4oz butter, chilled

For the stock

600ml 1pt water
bay leaf
1 sliced onion

1 chicken stock cube
1 stick celery
sprig parsley

1 Simmer all stock ingredients together with the neck and duck giblets (but not the liver) for one hour.
2 Remove any discoloured parts from livers. Fry briefly in a little butter until just firm.
3 Set oven to 220°C/425°F/Mark 7.
4 Prick ducks all over to pierce the skin. Salt them lightly.
5 Put them on a rack over a roasting tin, lying breast side down. Roast for one and a half hours, turning over at half-time. (One and a quarter hours for smaller ducks, two hours for larger ones.)
6 When stock has simmered for an hour, skim off scum and fat and strain into a clean saucepan. Add the unpeeled garlic, sugar or jam, half the blackcurrants, and the port. Simmer slowly until reduced to about 300ml/½pt.
7 When ducks are cooked (the juices from the thigh, if pierced, should run out clear) carefully lift them out and tip the juices from inside the ducks into the stock. Tip away all the fat from the roasting tin, but add any unfatty juices to the saucepan. Put the ducks on serving dishes.
8 Add livers to the saucepan.
9 Strain the sauce, pressing the garlic, livers and blackcurrants well to push their flesh through the sieve. Return to the saucepan, and skim off any surface fat, or blot the surface with absorbent kitchen paper to lift it.
10 Cut the butter into small dice and, over moderate heat, whisk the

pieces one by one into the sauce. Add the remaining whole blackcurrants.

Petits Pots au Café

450ml ¾pt milk
450ml ¾pt cream
50g 2oz caster sugar

6 egg yolks
2 eggs
1tbsp coffee essence

1   Set oven to 150°C/300°F/Mark 2.
2   Bring milk, cream and sugar to boiling point, stirring occasionally.
3   Beat eggs and yolks, add scalded milk, stirring. Strain.
4   Add coffee essence. Pour into little pots or ramekins. Cover with foil. Bake for 30–40 minutes, or until set. Allow to cool.

MENU 18

AVOCADO AND TOMATO SALAD
CHICKEN SMITANE
FLOATING ISLANDS

Introduction

The simple, colourful starter is followed by chicken in lemon and soured cream, and a light but spectacular pudding. The recipe for the chicken specifies removing the cooked chicken from the bones – not strictly necessary, but nice for the guests if you have the time.

Cook's gear

A large frying pan or sauté pan for cooking the floating islands, a perforated spoon for lifting them out and a clean tea-towel (not paper) for draining them.

Cook's tips

Beware of fibrous avocado pears that discolour easily. The stalk end is the tell-tale area – cut one open and have a look. The flesh should be clear, smooth and bright yellow with a green border under the skin.

The addition of mozzarella cheese or goat's milk cheese to the salad is good, but would add too many dairy products to this meal.

The trick with the floating islands is hardly to cook them at all: too much simmering and they become horribly rubbery. To prevent a skin forming on the custard cover closely, while still hot, with poly-wrap.

Getting ahead

The avocado salad cannot be made much more than two hours ahead of time, but the tomatoes can be skinned and the dressing made.

The chicken can be made the day before, but take care reheating. It is best to keep the sauce separate, and reheat meat and sauce separately, then tip off any juice or fat from the chicken and add the sauce – otherwise it may end up too runny.

66

The islands can be made in advance. One day is fine, more than that and sugar syrup runs from them – which doesn't perhaps matter. The custard may need rewhisking to smoothness if made in advance.

Vegetable or salad?
Something crunchy would be a good contrast to the smooth chicken – perhaps fried rice with chopped celery in it, with a salad of Webb or iceberg lettuce to follow.

Tomato and Avocado Salad

1kg   2lb large ripe tomatoes
3 large avocado pears
6tbsp olive oil
2tbsp white wine vinegar

salt and black pepper
1tbsp fresh basil, chopped
black olives

1   Dip tomatoes into boiling water for five seconds. Take them out, peel them. Slice thickly, discard stalk end.
2   Halve, peel and slice avocados.
3   Arrange tomato and avocado slices alternately on a flat dish.
4   Combine dressing ingredients in a screw-top jar. Shake well.
5   Spoon dressing over salad. Scatter black olives on top.

Chicken Smitane

2 large chickens, jointed
3 small lemons, squeezed
85g 3oz butter
1 litre 2pt chicken stock

sea salt and black pepper
2tbsp flour
150ml ¼pt soured cream

1 Skin joints and rub with lemon.
2 Melt butter in a sauté pan. Brown chicken pieces all over, a few at a time. Put them all back in the pan.
3 Add the stock. Season with salt and pepper. Cover pan. Bring to boil and simmer for 40 minutes or until chicken is tender.
4 Remove bones from chicken flesh. Put flesh in warmed serving dish.
5 Mix lemon juice with flour and soured cream.
6 Gradually add 600ml/1pt of the stock. Stir over moderate heat until slightly thickened. Simmer for 2–3 minutes, stirring.
7 Check seasoning. Pour some sauce over chicken, serve the rest separately.

Floating Islands

600ml 1pt milk
300ml ½pt cream
3tsp caster sugar
1tsp vanilla essence or vanilla pod
3tsp cornflour

6 egg yolks
4 egg whites
pinch of salt
140g 5oz caster sugar
30g 1oz grated chocolate

1 Slowly bring to boil half the milk, the cream, sugar and the vanilla. If using vanilla pod infuse for 30 minutes, then remove pod.
2 Mix cornflour with a little water. Add tablespoon of milk mixture, stir well and pour back into rest of milk mixture. Bring to boil over gentle heat, stirring continuously. Simmer for four minutes.
3 Beat egg yolks. Add milk mixture, beating. This should become thick enough to coat the back of a spoon – if it does not, stir over gentle heat, without boiling, until thicker. Strain into wide shallow dish. Cover with plastic film, and allow to cool.
4 Heat remaining milk in a deep frying pan with 1 pint of water.
5 Whisk egg whites with salt until stiff. Gradually whisk in sugar until very smooth, thick and shiny.

6 Cook spoonfuls of the meringue in the simmering milk and water for no more than 30 seconds on each side. They double in size, so cook only three at one time.
7 Lift out with perforated spoon and drain on a cloth. Cool. Lay 'islands' on custard 'lake'. Sprinkle with chocolate.

MENU 19

NETTLE AND LETTUCE SOUP
BABOTIE
CHOCOLATE PROFITEROLES

Introduction
Nettle soup is surprisingly good. Babotie is a mildly curried rich meat loaf from South Africa, and profiteroles are, I am told, every restaurant's most popular pudding. If you prefer the chocolate in the form of hot sauce, dust the buns with icing sugar, and melt the chocolate dipping ingredients with two tablespoons of golden syrup and serve hot.

Cook's gear
Rubber gloves for handling the nettles. A mincer for the babotie.

A piping bag and nozzles (large for the buns, narrow for filling them) for the profiteroles.

Cook's tips
Use only young nettles for the soup, handling with gloves until they are in the pot. If you cannot get nettles, substitute spinach or kale. Liquidize for a velvet, more elegant, texture.

To get the consistency and spice of the babotie just right, fry a teaspoon of the mixture before baking the lot.

For the profiteroles ginger-flavoured cream is a good variation.

In the absence of a piping bag for filling the profiteroles, cut them in half and dip the tops in chocolate before sandwiching tops and bottoms with cream.

Getting ahead
Make the soup up to two days ahead. Keep refrigerated.

Make the babotie up to two days ahead. Keep refrigerated. The empty cooked buns for the profiteroles may be frozen. Thaw, fill and coat with chocolate up to eight hours ahead.

Vegetable or salad?

Buttered rice with the babotie would be good. Serve any green salad.

Nettle and Lettuce Soup

500g	1lb young nettle leaves	50g	2oz butter
100g	4oz outer lettuce leaves	1tbsp	flour
250g	8oz potatoes, peeled	1.5l	3pt chicken stock
1	large onion		salt and pepper

1   Wash and destalk nettles and lettuce. Chop or shred fairly small.
2   Dice potatoes. Slice onion.
3   Melt butter. Add the onion. Cover and cook on low heat until onion is soft.
4   Add nettles and lettuce. Stir over moderate heat until reduced in bulk.
5   Add flour. Cook for 30 seconds, stirring.
6   Add stock and potatoes. Bring to boil stirring. Simmer for 15 minutes.
7   When potatoes are soft, check seasoning. Serve.

Babotie

2 slices crustless bread	2tsp seedless raisins
600ml 1pt milk	2tbsp lemon juice
2 dessert apples, chopped	1kg 2lb cooked lamb,
2 onions, finely chopped	minced
50g 2oz butter	salt and pepper
1tbsp curry powder	4 eggs
2tbsp mango chutney	lemon or lime leaves (optional)
2tbsp almonds	

1   Set oven to 180°C/350°F/Mark 4.
2   Soak bread in milk.
3   Cook chopped apple and onion slowly in butter until soft.
4   Add curry powder and cook for further minute.
5   Add chutney, almonds, raisins and lemon juice.
6   Squeeze milk from bread. Put milk to one side.
7   Fork bread into meat. Mix in the curry sauce. Check seasoning.
8   Spread mixture in lightly greased pie dish. Bake for 15 minutes to form a skin.

9   Mix eggs with the milk and season well. Pour over meat. Top with lemon leaves.
10 Return to oven. Bake for 35 minutes or until top is slightly browned and set.

Chocolate Profiteroles

Choux pastry

85g 3oz butter	pinch of salt
200ml ⅓pt water	3 large eggs
100g 4oz plain flour	

Topping and filling

300ml ½pt double cream, whipped and sweetened	15g ½oz butter
175g 6oz dark sweetened chocolate	4tbsp water

1   Set oven to 200°C/400°F/Mark 6.
2   Heat butter and water together, ensuring that butter has completely melted before water boils.
3   As water boils furiously, tip in flour and salt. Remove pan from heat and immediately beat until flour is incorporated and mixture leaves sides of pan.
4   Allow to cool.
5   Gradually beat in two eggs and enough of the third one to give a smooth mixture which will drop, rather than run, off a spoon.
6   Pipe or put small teaspoons of the mixture well apart on a wet baking sheet.
7   Bake for 30 minutes or until risen, firm and fairly brown.
8   Dry the insides by making a pea-sized hole in the bottom of each profiterole and returning to oven (upside down) for five minutes.
9   Cool on wire rack. When cold fill with cream using a piping bag and narrow nozzle inserted through hole.
10 Gently melt chocolate with butter and water. Stir until smooth and shiny. Cool until warm.
11 Dip profiteroles deeply into chocolate. Allow to cool.

MENU 20

ARNOLD BENNETT EGGS
QUAILS WITH GRAPES
GREEN FRUIT SALAD WITH GINGER

Introduction

The eggs are really easy to manage providing you take the kitchen timer into the sitting room to summon everyone when they are ready. The quails make fingerbowls a necessity – no one can get the flesh off a quail's leg with knife and fork. The green fruit salad looks best in a clear glass bowl.

Cook's gear

Ramekins for the eggs.
   Melon baller for the fruit salad.

Cook's tips

In the absence of a second oven or warming drawer the eggs can be cooked in a roasting pan of hot water on the cooker top. Cover with foil and keep the water simmering for 6–7 minutes.

   Buy two quails per person unless they are unusually plump ones, or unless you buy them boned and stuff with a pork sausagemeat mixture, which is good too.

   Get small eggs for the starter, as fresh as possible. Fresh eggs, when broken onto a plate, have the white close around the yolk. Stale eggs have runny whites that flow all over the plate.

   Avoid cream with the fruit salad if you can. It appears, albeit in tiny quantities, in both first and second courses.

Getting ahead

The eggs can be prepared ready for baking the day before, and covered in poly-wrap until 12 minutes before dinner time.

   The quails should not be cooked too far in advance as they dry out easily. Arrange matters so the sauce is finished not more than thirty minutes before dinner; keep the quails warm in a gentle hot cupboard.

73

Vegetable or salad?

As the cook is going to have enough to do with eggs and the quails, a simple vegetable purée which can be re-heated while the eggs are in the oven would be best. Perhaps a well-buttered purée of cooked peas flavoured with garlic and mint in one side of a shallow dish, and a purée of well-cooked carrots flavoured with a little nutmeg or coriander on the other side. Have the purées meet diagonally in the middle of the dish, make sure the tops are flat, and mark them with a fork. Brush with butter, and reheat covered with foil, or in a microwave oven, covered in poly-wrap.

Arnold Bennett Eggs

250g 8oz smoked haddock
   fillet
milk for poaching fish
butter for greasing ramekins

2 tomatoes
8 eggs
8tbsp double cream
freshly ground pepper

1 Poach haddock in milk for 4–5 minutes. Flake the fish.
2 Butter eight ramekins. Divide the haddock between them.
3 Peel tomatoes. (Dip in boiling water for a few seconds to loosen skins.) Remove seeds. Roughly chop flesh and add to ramekins.
4 Break an egg into each ramekin. Cover with a tablespoonful of cream.
5 Season with pepper only, as fish will be salty.
6 Stand dishes in roasting pan of boiling water.
7 Bake for 12 minutes in the same oven as the quails (200°C/400°F/ Mark 6).
8 Serve at once.

Quails with Grapes

16 plump quails
8 rashers rindless, streaky
   bacon
2 small onions, chopped
bay leaf
parsley
6tbsp white wine

2tsp flour
300ml ½pt stock
250g 8oz seedless grapes or
   halved and seeded grapes
50g 2oz walnuts
1tbsp raisins
2tbsp double cream

1 Set oven to 200°C/400°F/Mark 6.
2 Cover each quail breast with half a rasher of bacon.
3 Bake uncovered for 15 minutes with the onion, bay leaf, parsley and white wine.
4 Remove bacon, bake for further 10 minutes, and keep birds warm on serving dish.
5 Skim fat from roasting tin. Whisk in flour.
6 Add stock and whisk until boiling. Strain into saucepan.
7 Check seasoning. Add grapes, walnuts and raisins. Reheat. Add cream. Spoon sauce over quails or serve separately.

Green Fruit Salad with Ginger

250g 8oz granulated sugar
600ml 1pt water
3tbsp lemon juice
4tbsp ginger wine

1.5kg 3lb any green fruit: melon, kiwi fruit, green apples, greengages, whole gooseberries and seedless grapes

1 Put sugar and water in heavy bottomed saucepan. Bring to the boil slowly. Once sugar has melted, turn up heat and boil fast until syrup is tacky. Allow to cool. Add lemon juice and ginger wine.
2 Prepare fruit; scoop melon into balls, slice peeled kiwi, slice apples (with skin left on) etc. Drop into the syrup to prevent discoloration.
3 Chill before serving.

MENU 21

TABBOULEH
MOUSSAKA
MARMALADE TART

Introduction
Tabbouleh is one of those nutritious and fresh Middle-Eastern salads, tasting strongly of lemon and mint. It is followed by moussaka and then a classic English marmalade tart.

Cook's gear
Teatowel or cloth for drying the burghul.
Large shallow flan ring or loose-bottomed flan tin for the tart.

Cook's tips
Burghul wheat (also called bulgar) can be bought from Greek or Lebanese food shops.
Dip the tomatoes in boiling water for a few seconds before skinning.
Treacle (or rather golden syrup) is the more usual tart filling, or marmalade and syrup can be mixed half and half.

Getting ahead
The wheat can be soaked a day in advance, and the ingredients prepared. Keep in separate bowls, covered tightly, in the refrigerator. Mix together just before serving; the cucumber will lose its juices, spoiling the dressing, if it is in contact with the salt in the salad for long.
The moussaka can be made the day before.
Make the tart up to five days ahead, but rewarm very slightly before serving – boiling marmalade is dangerously hot.

Vegetable or salad?
Serve a green salad with a light dressing made with the smallest amount of oil but with plenty of lemon juice and herbs to cut through the richness of the moussaka.

76

Tabbouleh

250g 8oz burghul or fine
    cracked wheat
175g 6oz spring onions,
    chopped
175g 6oz fresh parsley,
    chopped
175g 6oz tomatoes, skinned
    and chopped

100g 4oz cucumber, diced
    finely without peeling
4tbsp fresh mint, chopped
6tbsp lemon juice
6tbsp olive oil
salt and pepper
about 30 small crisp cos lettuce
    leaves

1 Soak cracked wheat for about one hour in cold water. Drain and squeeze dry in a clean teatowel. Spread over tray to dry for an hour.
2 Shortly before serving mix everything together except the lettuce leaves.
3 Put a small helping of tabbouleh on each plate, with 3 or 4 lettuce leaves for scooping up the salad.

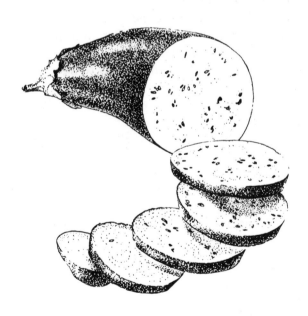

Moussaka

750g 1½lb aubergines, sliced
2 onions, finely chopped
1kg 2lb minced lamb
oil for frying
2 cloves garlic, crushed
1kg 2lb tinned tomatoes
300ml ½pt white wine
2tbsp tomato purée
pinch of nutmeg
salt, pepper

2 potatoes, thinly sliced
30g 1oz butter
30g 1oz flour
600ml 1pt milk
2tbsp cream
2 egg yolks
100g 4oz Cheddar cheese, grated
2tbsp dried breadcrumbs

1 Sprinkle aubergine slices with salt to extract bitter juices. Leave for half an hour.
2 Fry onion and then the lamb in hot oil, a small quantity at a time. Remove from pan.
3 Fry garlic for 30 seconds, then add tomatoes and their juice.
4 Add wine, tomato purée, nutmeg, salt and pepper. Bring to boil and simmer for few minutes.
5 Put back lamb and onion. Cover and simmer gently until sauce has thickened and meat is tender (about 40 minutes).
6 Set oven to 200°C/400°F/Mark 6.
7 Rinse salt off aubergines and pat dry. Fry to light brown on both sides. Fry potato slices similarly.
8 Put meat mixture in a casserole with a central layer of aubergine and potato slices.
9 Melt butter, stir in flour. Add milk. Stir until boiling. Add cream. Allow to cool slightly.
10 Beat in egg yolks and half the cheese.
11 Pour sauce over moussaka. Sprinkle with remaining cheese and the breadcrumbs.
12 Bake for 35 minutes or until top is brown and bubbling.

Marmalade Tart

For the pastry
500g 1lb plain flour
pinch of salt
300g 10oz butter
1tbsp caster sugar

2 egg yolks
squeeze of lemon juice
6tbsp icy water

For the filling
500g   1lb not-too-chunky
   marmalade

juice of one orange
2 cups fresh white
   breadcrumbs

To serve
whipped cream

1   Set oven to 190°C/375°F/Mark 5.
2   Sift flour with salt. Rub in the butter. Fork in sugar and egg yolks mixed with lemon juice and half the water. If the pastry is too dry and crumbly add remaining water in stages but take care not to over-work the pastry or to get it too wet. Chill.
3   Roll out two-thirds of the pastry to line 30cm/12in flan ring. Prick base with fork. Fill case with even layer of breadcrumbs.
4   Warm the marmalade with orange juice until smooth and liquid. Pour into the pastry case without disturbing the layer of crumbs.
5   Lattice the top with strips of pastry cut from the trimmings and remaining dough.
6   Bake until pastry is brown at edges. Allow to cool to luke-warm before serving with whipped cream handed separately.

MENU 22

SOUPE AU PISTOU
DUCK BREASTS WITH PEPPERCORNS
PASSIONFRUIT CREAM

Introduction

This menu is for the keen cook – it requires a good twenty minutes in the kitchen while everyone else is having a drink. But it is one of those truly sensational, and horribly expensive (you are left with eight duck legs which must be frozen for another occasion – see menu 51) dishes that get Michelin stars for restaurants. However, the soup (usually a great peasant main course, here a smaller more refined version) and the fruit cream can be prepared well in advance.

Cook's gear

A pestle and mortar or liquidizer or processor for the pistou.

2 heavy based frying pans for cooking the duck. Best of all are the ones with a griddle base – they give the duck steak attractive brand marks. A really hot grill will do too – brush the breast with butter before grilling.

Tall very thin glasses for the passionfruit cream.

Cook's tips

If you have no fresh basil, use a small jar of pistou (pesto).

Wrap the duck legs individually before freezing them so they need not all be thawed at once.

If the ducks have a thick layer of fat under the skin, you can scrape it off before frying the crisp skin.

Tinned passionfruit pulp is not as delicious as fresh flesh, but it is pretty good. Go easy on the sugar, however – it is generally already sweetened.

Do not be tempted to strain out the passionfruit seeds; they are part of the charm.

80

Getting ahead

The soup can be made in advance and frozen, or made a few days ahead and refrigerated.

The duck stock reduction and the turnips can be prepared the day before the dinner, but most of the work is, sadly, last-minute.

The fruit cream is best made six hours ahead.

Vegetable or salad?

The turnips, coming after all the vegetables in the soup, will do adequately, but perhaps a salad, especially if it contained cooked mangetout peas, or even tinned French petits pois, with lettuce and plenty of mint and parsley, would go well with the duck.

Soupe au Pistou

350g 12oz potatoes, peeled and diced
3 leeks, finely sliced
3 carrots, finely sliced
3tbsp olive oil
350g 12oz dried haricot beans, soaked overnight

175g 6oz green beans, sliced
1.5l 3pt chicken stock
sea salt and black pepper
1tbsp vermicelli pasta
4 ripe tomatoes, peeled and chopped

For the pistou
6 garlic cloves, crushed
6tbsp fresh basil, chopped

4tbsp olive oil

To serve
85g 3oz grated Gruyère cheese

1 Cook the potatoes, leeks and carrots slowly in the oil until softened.
2 Add haricot beans, green beans, stock, salt and pepper. Simmer until haricot beans are soft (about 1½ hours).
3 Add pasta and tomatoes – cook 3–4 minutes until pasta is just tender.
4 Liquidize or pound together garlic and basil to a paste. Add oil drop by drop, mixing continuously, to make an emulsion.
5 Just before serving stir pistou into soup. Hand cheese separately.

Duck Breasts with Green Peppercorns

4 plump young 2.5kg/5lb
   ducklings
few slices celery, carrot, onion
   and leek, sprig of parsley
few black peppercorns
4tbsp green peppercorns,
   frozen or tinned

100g 4oz butter
4tbsp cream
16 tiny round turnips with
   stalk intact
salt

1　Lift breasts from the birds by cutting down each side of breastbone
   and easing away flesh. Sever as close as possible to wing joint to get
   the maximum amount of breast. Take off legs for some later dish,
   and put carcasses, but not the skin or fatty parts near the tail, into a
   large saucepan with vegetable slices, parsley and black peppercorns.
2　Cover with water and simmer gently for three or four hours to
   reduce and strengthen the stock, skimming off scum and fat
   occasionally. Strain the stock, make sure it is absolutely fat free,
   then boil it down to no more than 150ml/¼pt.
3　Peel turnips but leave each with 2.5cm/1in of green stalk. Boil in
   salted water until just tender, drain and set aside.
4　20 minutes before serving, heat a heavy frying pan and put in duck
   breasts, skin side down without any fat. Cook over moderate heat
   for 10 minutes, then take out, pull off and reserve skins and fry the
   breasts, the other way up for another five minutes or so. Remove to
   a serving platter, cover and keep warm.
5　Reheat turnips, cover and keep warm too.
6　Cut duck skins into strips and put back in pan, pale side down, to
   fry until crisp all through. Take out, drain on absorbent paper and
   sprinkle with a little salt.
7　Pour off the fat from pan but do not wash it. Put into it the reduced
   duck stock and green peppercorns (rinsed if tinned). Boil up and
   add butter, bit by bit, whisking and swirling the pan to incorporate
   it evenly. Add cream, boil up again and pour round the duck
   breasts. Surround with the turnips, stalk side up, and scatter the
   crisp skin pieces on top.

Passionfruit Cream

36 passionfruit
3tbsp sweet sherry
300ml ½pt double cream
1 egg white
2tbsp sugar

1 Scoop out passionfruit flesh. Mix with sherry. Divide between eight glasses.
2 Whip cream until stiff. Whisk egg white with sugar until stiff and fold into cream.
3 Put a large spoonful into each glass. Chill.

MENU 23

EGGS TAPENADE
CALVES' LIVER AND SPINACH FEUILLETÉE
MANGO AND DATE SALAD

Introduction

Regrettably the main course of this menu requires the last-minute frying of the calves' liver; it toughens and spoils if cooked in advance. But the first course is cold, prepared ahead of time, as is the dessert.

Cook's gear

A piping bag and large fluted nozzle for the eggs (optional). The tapenade can be prepared in the traditional way with a pestle and mortar or in a food processor or liquidizer.

Cook's tips

Tell the butcher to skin the calves' liver for you, and to make sure it has no tubes or sinews in it. Unless he is skilled, slice the liver yourself — inexperienced butcher's boys frequently give you a slice like a doorstep one side and paper-thin the other. You are after even thin mini-slices.

To see if the mangoes are ripe, smell them — they should be perfumed, and feel a little soft, without being squashy to the touch.

Getting ahead

The eggs can be prepared, but not filled, the day before.

Fill them up to six hours before dinner. Keep covered with poly-wrap to prevent drying out, until half an hour before serving (remove the plastic then — eggs taste of plastic if served immediately they are unwrapped).

The pastry case can be cooked the day before, as can the spinach. But the liver and sauce are last minute matters.

The assembled 'vol au vent' can be left in a warm oven while you eat the first course.

The mangoes are best sliced on the day of serving. Keep covered tightly in the refrigerator or the milk and butter will taste of mango.

84

Vegetable or salad?

The pastry will provide starch and the spinach greenery, so a leafy salad with a bit of bite to it – perhaps provided by spring onions or radishes – would do, to be served after, rather than with, the feuilletée.

Eggs Tapenade

8 eggs
50g 2oz anchovy fillets soaked in milk for 10 minutes
85g 3oz black olives, stoned
85g 3oz capers

50g 2oz tuna, drained
1tsp mustard powder
150ml ¼pt olive oil
1tbsp brandy
pepper, cloves and nutmeg
fresh parsley, chopped

To serve
toast and butter

1 Hard boil eggs, cool and shell.
2 Drain anchovies.
3 Blend them together with olives, capers, tuna and mustard until smooth.
4 Add oil gradually, beating between additions, as if making mayonnaise.
5 Stir in brandy and spices.
6 Halve eggs lengthwise. Scoop out yolks and mash to smooth paste with tapenade. Moisten with extra oil if necessary.
7 Fill whites with mixture. Sprinkle with parsley. Serve with fingers of hot toast.

Calves' Liver and Spinach Feuilletée

500g 1lb puff pastry (frozen is fine)
beaten egg
500g 1lb fresh young spinach, washed and de-stalked
pepper, salt and nutmeg
750g 1½lb best calves' liver

50g 2oz butter for frying
15g ½oz flour
3tbsp madeira
150ml ¼pt beef stock
100g 4oz butter for the sauce, chilled and cut into small cubes

1 Set oven to 230°C/450°F/Mark 8.
2 Roll the pastry into two large rounds about the thickness of a coin, and rather bigger than a dinner plate. Put a plate over each piece as a guide and cut round with a knife. Prick one of the rounds all over with a fork and lay it on a wet baking tray.
3 Using a smaller plate or a large saucer as a guide, cut through the second pastry round so you have an outer ring and an inner circle.
4 Brush the large complete round with beaten egg, taking care not to wet the cut edges, then lay the ring of pastry cut from the other round on top of it, like a border. Brush with egg, again **taking** care not to go over the cut edges, which would prevent rising.
5 Mark the smaller round with the back of a knife in a criss-cross pattern and brush it with beaten egg too. Lay on another wet baking tray, or beside the larger pastry if there is room. Prick all over with a fork.
6 Bake until the pastry case is well risen and very dark brown (about 20 minutes). If the middle of the large round has risen, push it down gently with a fist while it is still warm.
7 Cook the spinach until just limp in boiling water. Drain well, and pat dry with cloth or paper. Toss in a little melted butter. Return to a saucepan for later reheating. Sprinkle with pepper, salt and nutmeg.
8 Ten minutes before serving, put the pastry case and lid in the oven to reheat.
9 Slice the liver into thin scallopini. Just before serving, fry the liver (patted dry with paper or cloth to prevent splattering) fast in butter, until just firm and still pink inside – cut one open to see, if unsure. Lift out of pan to prevent overcooking.
10 Melt about a tablespoon of butter in the pan. Add the flour. Scrape up any stuck particles from the pan bottom. Add the stock and madeira and boil fast until you have a syrupy sauce.
11 With the sauce just bubbling whisk in the chilled butter cubes, one by one, to form a creamy emulsion. Set aside.
12 Reheat the spinach, and spread in the pastry case. Then add the liver. Put onto a heated serving dish. Pour over the sauce, put the lid in place and serve.

Mango and Date Salad

6 perfect ripe mangoes   juice of 1 orange
1 punnet fresh dates

1   Peel and slice the mangoes into a bowl.
2   De-stone the dates and cut them in half. Add them with the orange
    juice to the bowl. Chill before serving.

MENU 24

RICH MUSHROOM AND PARSLEY SOUP
CHICKEN CURRY WITH YOGHURT
TANGERINES IN CARAMEL SAUCE

Introduction

The mushroom soup, which owes much to Elizabeth David, is very aromatic and rich. The chicken curry, by contrast, is light and spicy, and the tangerines tart and fresh. Try to avoid serving cream with them.

Cook's gear

Liquidizer for the soup.

Heavy small pan for making syrup. In the absence of one, cover the sugar with a few spoons of water, then boil to caramel – it is less inclined to burn this way in a thin pan.

Cook's tips

Do not bother to chop or slice the mushrooms and parsley too well – the soup goes through the liquidizer later.

The yoghurt is inclined to curdle. If you mind this, mix it with a level teaspoon of cornflour before adding it to the sauce.

Getting ahead

The soup can be made up to two days in advance and kept refrigerated.

The curry, without the yoghurt, can be cooked two days ahead. Add the yoghurt when reheating.

The caramel sauce can be made a week ahead, but do not peel the tangerines or immerse them in the sauce until the day of the party. They benefit from a few hours in the sauce, however.

Vegetable or salad?

Boiled or fried rice would be good, but so would fresh corn *off* the cob. Or what about Greek pitta bread, damped and stuffed with a mixed purée of mashed potato and carrot, then wrapped in foil and heated, and cut across in slices to be eaten as a 'vegetable' with the curry. A salad of red lettuce (radicchio) would be pretty and refreshing after the chicken.

Rich Mushroom and Parsley Soup

100g 4oz butter
2 cloves garlic, crushed
750g 1½lb flat mushrooms, roughly chopped
100g 4oz parsley leaves

5 slices crustless white bread
1 litre 2pts good chicken stock
salt and pepper
nutmeg or ground mace
300ml ½pt cream

1 Melt butter, add garlic, mushrooms and parsley. Stir.
2 Cover saucepan and cook slowly for 10 minutes.
3 Crumble bread into pan. Add stock and seasonings.
4 Heat, stirring. Simmer for 10 minutes.
5 Liquidize the soup. Pour into a clean saucepan and add the cream. Reheat without boiling.

Chicken Curry with Yoghurt

100g 4oz flour
½tsp each: turmeric, cayenne,
   dry English mustard, crushed
   coriander
2 chickens
4tbsp oil
2 large onions, sliced
2 cloves garlic
1tbsp curry powder

600ml 1pt chicken stock
1 bay leaf
1tbsp fresh mint, chopped
1tbsp tomato purée
juice of 2 small lemons
salt and pepper
4tbsp yoghurt
2tbsp flaked almonds

1 Set oven to 180°C/350°F/Mark 4.
2 Mix flour with first four spices.
3 Joint each chicken into eight pieces. Roll in seasoned flour.
4 Heat oil. Brown chicken on all sides, a few pieces at a time. Lift out and put into a roasting tin.
5 Fry onions slowly in the oil until soft. Add garlic and curry powder. Cook for two minutes.
6 Add stock, bay leaf, mint, tomato purée and lemon juice. Bring to boil, stirring. Check seasoning.
7 Pour sauce over chicken joints. Cover with foil. Bake 50–60 minutes or until chicken is tender. Skim off any fat.
8 Lift chicken onto serving dish. Add yoghurt and almonds to sauce in roasting tin. Reheat without boiling. Pour over chicken.

Tangerines in Caramel Sauce

2–3 tangerines or satsumas per
   person
250g 8oz granulated sugar

300ml ½pt water
2tbsp Grand Marnier
(optional)

1 Remove peel and pith from tangerines. Keep the fruit whole.
2 Melt half the sugar slowly in a heavy saucepan.
3 When brown and bubbling add the water, standing well back because it will fizz dangerously.
4 Add remaining sugar. Bring to the boil, stirring.
5 Continue to boil until of a syrupy consistency. Allow to cool. Add the Grand Marnier and pour over tangerines.

MENU 25

CHICKEN LIVER AND CROÛTON SALAD
QUENELLES WITH CHABLIS SAUCE
CHERRY STRUDEL

Introduction
This dinner is definitely for the enthusiastic cook. It is not difficult or particularly time-consuming, but it does require a bit of organization and some last-minute work. It is extremely light and pretty, however, and well worth the trouble.

Cook's gear
Teatowel to roll up the strudel.

Cook's tips
Make sure the livers have any discoloured greenish or yellow patches cut away: they discolour from contact with the gall bladder, which makes the liver taste very bitter. Do not worry about pale livers however, they are generally richer and milder flavoured than dark ones.

Chilling the ingredients for the quenelles, and the butter for the sauce, prevents curdling.

To mould perfectly shaped quenelles, dip two dessert spoons in the hot broth before shaping.

If you don't want to taste the raw fish mixture to get the seasoning right, poach a spoonful, then taste it.

Unless you are very experienced do not attempt to make strudel pastry. It is fun, but takes a deal of rolling and pulling. Buy it (often called filo pastry) in Greek or continental food shops. Keep it covered with polywrap or a damp towel, or brushed with butter, while you work or it will dry out and crack.

Getting ahead
The salad leaves can be prepared the day before and kept in a

polythene bag, and the croûtons can be fried, cooled and kept in an airtight box. But the livers are last-minute matters.

The quenelle mixture can be made the day before, up to the point of adding the cream. The cream should go in on the day of the dinner. Poach a few hours before dinner, allow to cool, and reheat gently in the sauce.

The strudel can be made the day before but benefits from reheating to crispen the pastry layers before serving.

Vegetable or salad?

Most vegetables are too overpowering to go with such delicate fish. Stick to boiled rice or small peeled new potatoes (steamed or boiled) with a little butter and parsley. If you want a green vegetable, serve perfect sprigs of green broccoli as a separate course after the fish. No more salad, however.

Chicken Liver and Croûton Salad

2 thin slices crustless bread
250g 8oz mâche or lamb's
   lettuce
2 small radicchio, or hearts of
   two frilly endive
3 tbsp olive oil
2 tsp sherry vinegar

salt and pepper
350g 12oz cleaned chicken
   or duck livers
1 clove garlic, crushed
oil and butter for frying

1   Cut bread into small neat dice. Fry slowly so they brown evenly and right through in oil. Drain.
2   Tear the well washed and drained salad leaves into small pieces and toss gently in a dressing made from the olive oil and vinegar, salt and pepper.
3   Divide the salad between eight plates.
4   Slice each liver into two or three pieces, and smear lightly with crushed garlic.
5   Just before serving, heat a knob of butter until foaming and fry the livers as fast as you dare, browning first one side, then the other, until just firm – about 3 minutes in all. Lift out and scatter over each salad.
6   Toss the croûtons into the garlic-flavoured butter. Reheat very briefly, turning with a spoon. Sprinkle over the plates of salad. Serve at once.

Quenelles with Chablis Sauce

1kg 2lb salmon fillet, skinned
500g 1lb whiting fillet,
  skinned
4 slices white bread, crustless
milk

salt, pepper and cayenne
4 egg whites, chilled
450ml ¾pt double cream,
  chilled

For the stock
fish heads, skins and bones
1.5 litre 3pts water

bay leaf, parsley sprig, celery
  stick

For the sauce
100g 4oz butter, chilled and
  diced
30g 1oz flour

150ml ¼pt Chablis
150ml ¼pt double cream

1. Boil stock ingredients together for 20 minutes. Strain.
2. Mince fish fillets twice or blend in food processor.
3. Soak bread in milk. Squeeze dryish and beat into the fish. Season with pepper only.
4. Beat egg whites until just frothy and then gradually work them into the fish. Refrigerate for at least one hour.
5. Beat in the cream and season with salt and cayenne.
6. Heat the stock until simmering in shallow pan.
7. Mould the mixture into egg-shapes between two spoons and drop the quenelles gently into the liquid.
8. Poach for about eight minutes or until they are firm to the touch – take care not to overcook. Place on heated serving dish and keep warm.
9. Boil cooking stock rapidly until reduced to about 450ml/¾pt.
10. Melt a quarter of the butter. Stir in flour, cook for 30 seconds. Add wine and stock. Stir until boiling then boil fast until reduced to 300ml/½pt.
11. Keep the sauce boiling gently and beat in the butter pieces bit by bit to form an emulsion. Add the cream, and add salt to taste. Pour over quenelles just before serving.

Cherry Strudel

750g 1½lb fresh cherries,
   stoned
100g 4oz granulated sugar
50g 2oz demerara sugar
1tsp ground cinnamon

4tbsp dried breadcrumbs,
   toasted brown
100g 4oz melted butter
4 large sheets of filo pastry
icing sugar
double cream for serving

1   Set oven to 190°C/375°F/Mark 5.
2   Stew cherries over low heat in pan with two tablespoons of granulated sugar.
3   When soft, pour off liquid. Mix cherries with remaining granulated sugar, all the demerara sugar, cinnamon, breadcrumbs and half the melted butter.
4   Lay one very large teatowel or two smaller ones put side by side and overlapping on the worktop. They must cover an area of about 60cm × 40cm/24in × 15in. Lay the strudel leaves on this, overlapping them so that the filling will not seep through the joins. Four sheets of filo should ensure that most of the area is covered in two layers of pastry. Brush the leaves with melted butter as you go, then spread the cherry mixture evenly over the area, leaving a good 5cm/2in margin round the edge.
5   Fold in the edges – again to help keep in the filling – and roll up the strudel using the teatowel to support it as you roll. Ease onto a greased baking tray and brush with remaining melted butter.
6   Bake for about 20 minutes or until crisp and brown on top. Dust with icing sugar and serve hot or warm with sweetened whipped cream.

MENU 26

SPINACH ROLL
BRITTANY LAMB WITH HARICOT BEANS
KIWI AND MANGO SALAD

Introduction
A spinach roulade followed by lamb with beans may seem to be over-ambitious, but the recipes are simple enough, and providing second helpings of the first course are forbidden, the dinner, ending with a light sugarless fruit salad, should not be too heavy.

Cook's gear
Greaseproof paper and a large flat roasting tin for the spinach roll.

A pressure cooker speeds the bean cooking time to about 40 minutes, but is not necessary.

Cook's tips
Cool the roulade a little before rolling it up. It is easier to handle and nicer to eat.

If using a baking tray rather than a roasting tin, lay doubled greaseproof paper on it and fold and staple the edges to form 'walls' of 2.5cm/1in high.

A meat thermometer is a good gadget if you want to catch your lamb just pink – it is just right at 165°C/330°F. Allow 20 minutes for the meat to rest after coming out of the oven; it will not cool noticeably, but will have an even colour right through and will be easier to carve.

Getting ahead
The roll should, ideally, be baked shortly before serving – it is then at its best and puffiest. But it can be prebaked, rolled, and reheated once the lamb is out of the oven if there is not room for lamb and baking tray to be in there together. If this is done, a thin cheese sauce should be served with the roll to counteract any drying out caused by double-baking.

95

The beans can be cooked the day before, or even two days before, or cooked and frozen. Reheat in a saucepan. Remember to keep a little bean liquid for the lamb gravy.

The salad can be prepared up to six hours ahead. Cover with poly-wrap to prevent the fruit tainting milk and butter in the refrigerator.

Vegetable or salad?

Nothing more than the beans is necessary, with spinach roll going before and a fruit salad after, but you might like to serve half-tomatoes (sprinkled with breadcrumbs and butter and baked until just soft) for their crunchiness and colour.

They reheat perfectly, and very quickly – they could go in under the spinach roll once the meat is out.

Spinach Roll

750g 1½lb fresh or frozen leaf spinach	6 eggs, separated
30g 1oz butter	salt, pepper and nutmeg
	50g 2oz Parmesan or strong Cheddar cheese, grated

For the filling

30g 1oz butter	150ml ¼pt milk
350g 12oz mushrooms, chopped	2tbsp cream
30g 1oz flour	2tbsp chopped parsley
	salt and pepper

1 Wash spinach, remove stalks. Put in pan without water. Cover and cook gently for 5–7 minutes. Drain by squeezing between two plates. Chop very finely. Mix in butter.
2 Set oven to 190°C/375°F/Mark 5.
3 Line a large roasting tin with a larger sheet of greaseproof paper. Brush the paper with oil or melted butter.
4 Beat egg yolks into spinach. Season with salt, pepper and nutmeg.
5 Whisk egg whites until stiff. Fold into spinach. Pour mixture into roasting tin, spread flat and sprinkle with half of the grated cheese. Bake for 10–15 minutes or until it feels dry to the touch.
6 Meanwhile make the filling: melt butter and in it fry mushrooms. Add flour, mix well. Add milk and bring to boil, stirring. Simmer until thick and creamy. Stir in cream and parsley. Season well.

7   Sprinkle rest of grated cheese onto a sheet of greaseproof paper placed on a tea-towel. Turn baked spinach out on to it, face downwards. Peel off backing paper.
8   Spread filling over top and roll up, removing the second piece of paper as you go. Serve on warm dish, whole or in slices.

Brittany Lamb with Haricot Beans

For the beans
1 carrot, sliced
3 shallots, chopped
30g   1oz butter
500g   1lb haricot beans,
   soaked overnight

1 onion, peeled and stuck with
   a clove
bouquet garni: sprig thyme,
   sprig parsley, bayleaf, celery
   stick, tied together

For the roast
3kg   6lb leg of lamb
2 cloves garlic

30g   1oz butter

To finish
1tbsp butter
1tbsp parsley, chopped

salt and pepper

1   Soften carrot and shallot in the butter over gentle heat in a covered pan. After 10 minutes add drained beans, onion and clove and the bouquet garni. Cover with fresh water, put on a lid, bring to boil and simmer for about two hours or until beans are soft – top up with water if necessary during cooking. Season with salt and pepper.
2   To roast lamb, set oven to 230°C/450°F/Mark 8. Make a few tiny cuts in lamb flesh and stick thin slivers of peeled garlic into them. Season lamb and smear with butter. Roast for 15 minutes. Turn oven down to 200°C/400°F/Mark 6 and roast for further 25 minutes per pound.
3   Liquidize a cupful of the cooked beans together with some of the juice and the onion (having removed the clove). Strain off the rest of bean liquid. Toss the beans in the creamy onion sauce from the liquidizer. Add the tablespoon of butter and chopped parsley.
4   Lift lamb onto a large serving dish with a good lip all round it. Tip beans round the lamb. Keep warm.

5   Skim fat from the roasting tin, add a wineglass of bean stock to tin. Boil up stirring in any sediment on bottom. Taste and season. Hand gravy separately.

Kiwi and Mango Salad

6 ripe mangoes   12 ripe but not squashy kiwi
                                              fruit

1   Peel the mangoes and cut them into bite-sized blocks.
2   Peel the kiwi and slice them across fairly thickly.
3   Mix the two fruits in a clear glass bowl.

MENU 27

ASPARAGUS AND PEA SOUP
CHICKEN WITH TARRAGON AND TOMATO
FROZEN STRAWBERRY CREAMS

Introduction
A light and velvety asparagus and pea soup, a tangy chicken casserole and a rich iced strawberry dessert is a good summer dinner menu. If the weather is wonderfully warm the soup can be served chilled, rather than hot as here. Even when in season, asparagus are expensive, so this recipe assumes tinned asparagus and frozen peas – no one would ever know.

Cook's gear
Liquidizer for the soup.
    Individual ramekins for the frozen creams.

Cook's tips
If using fresh asparagus, cook them in boiling water and use the water in the soup too. Liquidize and sieve (to remove fibrous threads).
    Other fruit – peaches, apricots, raspberries – can of course be substituted for the strawberries. Damsons are good, but should be cooked with sugar, stoned and sieved before folding into the cream.

Getting ahead
The soup can be made two days ahead and kept refrigerated.
    The chicken reheats well. Make the day before.
    The frozen creams should not be done more than a few days in advance – the cream can become streaky and icy.

Vegetable or salad?
Rice, noodles or mashed potatoes would be best for mopping up the sauce. Baked fennel or sticks of boiled salsify would have enough power not to be overwhelmed by the tomato sauce.

Asparagus and Pea Soup

1 litre   2pt chicken stock
2 tins asparagus (total weight
   1kg/2lb)
500g   1lb frozen peas

6 sprigs mint
salt and pepper
300ml   ½pt creamy milk

1   Bring stock to the boil with asparagus (and juice from cans), peas,
    mint leaves, salt and pepper.
2   Liquidize and reheat with the milk, without boiling.

Chicken with Tarragon and Tomato

2 chickens
flour seasoned with salt and
   pepper
olive oil for frying
1 medium aubergine
1 large onion, chopped
1kg   2lb tinned tomatoes
2tbsp tomato purée

2 cloves garlic
6 large sprigs French tarragon
bouquet garni: thyme, bay leaf,
   parsley, tied together
150ml   ¼pt dry white wine
300ml   ½pt chicken stock
salt and pepper

To serve
tarragon leaves, chopped

1   Joint chickens into eight pieces each. Roll in seasoned flour.
2   Slice aubergine thickly.
3   Heat a tablespoon of oil in frying pan. Fry chicken pieces until evenly browned. Lift into saucepan.
4   In a little more oil gently fry aubergine slices until brown on both sides. Add to saucepan.
5   Fry onion until soft. Add to chicken with tomatoes, tomato purée, garlic, tarragon sprigs (tied together with other herbs) and wine and stock. Cover saucepan and simmer for forty minutes or until chicken is tender.
6   Remove bunch of herbs. If sauce is too thin, remove chicken and boil the sauce fast until reduced and of syrupy consistency. Skim off any fat. Check seasoning, adding teaspoon of sugar if acidic.
7   Return chicken and heat through. Add chopped tarragon and serve.

Frozen Strawberry Creams

1kg   2lb   fresh strawberries   2tbsp kirsch or framboise
250g   8oz   icing sugar   600ml   1pt double cream

1   Purée or mash strawberries. Add sugar and alcohol.
2   Whip cream until very thick. Fold into purée.
3   Pour into ramekins. Freeze.
4   Remove from freezer half an hour before starting dinner.

MENU 28

SORREL AND CHEESE SOUFFLÉ
BRAISED OXTAIL
BROWN SUGAR MERINGUES WITH LEMON

Introduction

Sorrel gives a pretty colour and a slight tang to a cheese soufflé. The helpings should be small though, whatever the temptation, because there is a hefty stew to follow.

Similarly the meringues should be small and lemony – light enough to manage after the oxtail.

Cook's gear

Eight ramekins or two 15cm/6in soufflé dishes.
A piping bag with large fluted nozzle for the meringues (optional).
An electric whisk is useful for whisking the egg whites.

Cook's tips

Individual soufflés, baked in ramekins, are a good idea. They can be put in the oven 10 minutes before dinner and gauged more accurately than large soufflés.

Over-cooked and hence rather dry soufflés do not collapse like moist ones. To get the best of both worlds, over-cook large soufflés by fifteen minutes and small ones by five minutes and serve with a cheese sauce.

Ask the butcher for *ox*-tails. Cows' tails are thinner and scrawnier.

For toffee-ish meringues under-cook them slightly – but these will get soggy if done far in advance. Make on the day.

Ginger marmalade may be substituted for home-made lemon curd.

Getting ahead

Make the cheese and yolk base for the soufflés up to 2 days in advance. Rewarm slightly to loosen when adding whisked whites and baking.

Make the oxtail stew up to 2 days ahead and refrigerate but add flageolets only on reheating.

Make the meringues up to 2 weeks in advance if cooked until dry and store in airtight container. Make curd up to 1 month in advance – store in refrigerator.

Vegetable or salad?

Boiled potatoes are traditional but mashed ones take up the sauce better. Forget other vegetables – the stew is full of carrots and flageolets.

Sorrel and Cheese Soufflé

100g 4oz sorrel	300ml ½pt milk
350g 12oz spinach	50g 2oz strong Cheddar or
50g 2oz butter	Gruyère cheese, grated
50g 2oz flour	4 eggs, separated
pinch cayenne	1 extra egg white
½tsp mustard	2tsp Parmesan cheese, grated
salt and pepper	butter for greasing dishes

1   Set oven to 200°C/400°F/Mark 6 for large soufflés, 220°C/425°F/ Mark 7 for ramekins.
2   Remove stalks from sorrel and spinach. Wash leaves thoroughly.
3   Cook leaves for two minutes in boiling salted water. Drain. Press hard between two plates to extract water. Chop finely or liquidize.
4   Lightly butter two 15cm/6in soufflé dishes or eight individual ramekins.
5   Melt the 2oz of butter. Stir in flour and seasonings. Add milk, bring to boil, stirring. Boil for further minute.
6   Remove from heat. Add cheese, sorrel and spinach.
7   Mix in yolks. Whisk egg whites until stiff. Stir one spoonful into sorrel mixture. Fold in remaining egg white. Do not over-mix.
8   Pour into soufflé dishes/ramekins. Sprinkle with Parmesan. Bake large soufflés 25–30 minutes (ramekins 10–12 minutes.) Or until tops are brown and soufflés not too wobbly when given a sharp shove.

Braised Oxtail

16 large pieces oxtail
500g 1lb carrots, peeled and
    sliced
500g 1lb onions, sliced
2tbsp beef dripping
2tbsp flour
300ml ½pt red wine
2tbsp tomato purée

1 litre 2pt beef stock
bouquet garni: bay leaf, parsley
    stalks, thyme, celery stick –
    tied together
salt and pepper
1 large tin flageolet beans,
    rinsed and drained

1 Set oven to 150°C/300°F/Mark 2.
2 In large heavy pan brown oxtail and vegetables in hot fat. Do a few
   pieces at a time, and replace all when done.
3 Stir in flour.
4 Add wine, tomato purée and stock. Bring to boil, stirring.
5 Sink bouquet garni in liquid.
6 Season with salt and pepper. Cover tightly.
7 Bake for four hours or until meat is tender.
8 Lift oxtail and vegetables into serving dishes. Keep covered and
   warm.
9 Skim fat from liquid. Remove bouquet garni. Boil hard until
   reduced to a syrupy sauce.
10 Five minutes before serving add beans, check seasoning, and pour
    over oxtail.

Brown Sugar Meringues with Lemon

4 egg whites
100g 4oz caster sugar
100g 4oz soft brown sugar

oil and caster sugar for coating
foil

Filling
200ml ⅓pt double cream,
    whipped

4tbsp lemon curd (recipe
    below)

1 Set oven to 110°C/225°F/Mark 1/2.
2 Line two baking trays with foil. Brush with oil and lightly dust
   with caster sugar.
3 Whisk egg whites with both the sugars (except two tablespoons of

caster) until so stiff that the mixture will not flow at all when whisk is lifted.

4   Fold in remaining sugar.
5   Spoon (or pipe) mixture in rounds the size of a golf ball onto baking trays.
6   Bake for about two hours or until meringues are dry right through and can be easily removed from the foil (cook less for toffee-centred meringues). Allow to cool.
7   Sandwich with a mixture of whipped cream and lemon curd.

Lemon Curd

juice and finely grated rind of 2   250g   8oz sugar
  large lemons   3 eggs, beaten
85g   3oz butter

1   Stir everything together over gentle heat until thick. Strain and cool.

MENU 29

CARROT, MUSHROOM AND CUMIN SALAD
ROAST CARP WITH PEPPERS
FROZEN WHITE CHOCOLATE CREAM

Introduction

The frozen white chocolate is about the richest thing in this book, so it is important to precede it with fairly simple recipes – the salad is small and light, and the roast carp is pretty spectacular, but gastronomically plain.

Cook's gear

Swivel potato peeler for taking ribbon-strips from the carrots.

Large roasting tin big enough for the whole fish.

Ramekins for the frozen creams, with circles of foil or greaseproof paper lining the bases.

Cook's tips

Order the carp in good time from the fishmonger – they are not always easy to get, and disappear off the slab fast.

If the fish won't fit in the oven whole, decapitate it, cook the head separately, and stick it back in place on the serving dish covering the join with a tomato slice or two.

Of course the frozen mousse can be made with dark chocolate, and served with a white sauce – but it is more unusual this way round.

Getting ahead

The salad may be prepared 24 hours in advance: slice the celery and leave it in water. Prepare the carrots and put in a polythene bag. Make the dressing and toss the sliced mushrooms in it. Keep everything refrigerated.

Combine ingredients not more than an hour before dinner.

The fish can be prepared on the morning of the dinner, but cook it at the last moment – freshness is all.

The chocolate creams can be frozen up to a week before eating.

Vegetable or salad?

Fresh green peas.

Potatoes baked à la boulangère (sliced into a buttered dish, topped up with well-flavoured stock, and covered with breadcrumbs and a little grated cheese, then baked slowly until tender and brown) would be best, or the potatoes under the fish could be increased to 1kg/2lb. Don't worry about a salad – you have one as a starter.

Carrot, Mushroom and Cumin Salad

2 inner sticks celery
350g 12oz young carrots, peeled

350g 12oz very small white mushrooms

Dressing
3tbsp good salad oil
1tbsp lemon juice
1tsp ground cumin powder

½tsp made English mustard
salt and black pepper

To serve
hot buttered toast

1   Cut the celery into 5cm/2in lengths, then cut each piece lengthwise into the finest matchstick threads. Put into iced water and leave in the refrigerator for an hour – they will go attractively curly.
2   Using the potato peeler, strip the carrots into the finest ribbons.
3   Slice mushrooms finely.
4   Mix together the dressing ingredients. Toss vegetables and dressing together and arrange on eight plates.
5   Offer hot toast with the salad.

Roast Carp with Peppers

2kg 4lb whole carp
1tsp salt
100g 4oz streaky bacon
3 green peppers
3 tomatoes

500g 1lb boiled potatoes, sliced
300ml ½pt soured cream
100g 4oz melted butter
2tsp paprika
fresh parsley

1. Set oven to 180°C/350°F/Mark 4.
2. Clean carp and remove scales. Rub all over with salt. Cut evenly-spaced slits in the flesh and put slices of bacon, pepper and tomato in the openings.
3. Grease an ovenproof dish and arrange slices of potato in the bottom. Place carp on top.
4. Mix soured cream with melted butter and paprika and pour over fish. Bake, basting frequently, for about one hour. Garnish with plenty of chopped parsley.

Frozen White Chocolate Cream

4 eggs
100g 4oz caster sugar
250g 8oz best white chocolate

150ml ¼pt double cream
100g 4oz unsalted butter

For the sauce
175g 6oz good quality plain chocolate
2tbsp golden syrup

50g 2oz unsalted butter
1 teacup strong black coffee

1. Separate the eggs. Set a bowl over a saucepan of simmering water making sure the bottom of the bowl does not touch the water. In it whisk the yolks with the sugar until thick and mousse-like.
2. Put the white chocolate and the cream into a heavy saucepan over gentle heat and melt, stirring. Remove from the heat and add the butter, allowing it to melt into the chocolate.
3. Add the whisked sugar/yolk mixture, and stir occasionally until almost cool.
4. Whisk egg whites to a thick snow, fold into the chocolate, and pour the mixture into small ramekins, each with a circle of greaseproof paper or foil cut to fit the base. Freeze.
5. Put the sauce ingredients into a heavy pan and simmer, stirring until smooth.
6. When the chocolate creams are firm (they will not freeze rock-hard) run a knife round the sides and unmould them onto chilled plates. Remove the papers and return the creams to the freezer. Re-heat the sauce until smooth just before serving.

MENU 30

CUCUMBER AND CARAWAY ROAST VEAL WITH ROSEMARY GRAND MARNIER PANCAKES

Introduction
The starter of this menu is simplicity itself, as is the veal roast, but the pancakes take a bit of effort, skill and time.

There is some last minute cooking, but results are very professional.

Cook's gear
Omelette, crêpe or heavy frying pan for the pancakes.

Cook's tips
Sherry or tarragon vinegar are interesting alternatives to ordinary wine vinegar for the cucumber dish.

Slow roasting and frequent basting are important if the veal is not to dry out.

Getting ahead
The cucumber and tomato can be prepared up to 24 hours in advance, but the dish must be cooked at the last minute.

The veal should not be pre-roasted, but can be left to rest in a cool oven or warming drawer for half an hour.

The pancakes can be completed up to the grilling stage. Grilling should, ideally, be last minute so they arrive at the table sizzling. But they taste just the same if grilled before dinner.

Vegetable or salad?
Plain new potatoes or buttered noodles would be good.

Spinach, leaf or puréed with white sauce, is the classic vegetable for veal.

Cucumber and Caraway

50g 2oz butter
2tbsp wine vinegar
4 small tomatoes, peeled,
   seeded and cut into segments

2 cucumbers, peeled and cubed
1tbsp caraway seeds

1 Melt butter, add vinegar, vegetables and caraway seeds.
2 Toss over high heat for three minutes.
3 Season with salt and freshly ground black pepper. Serve piping hot
   but not over-cooked.

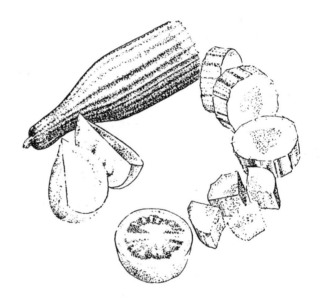

Roast Veal with Rosemary

1 medium onion, chopped
1 stick celery, chopped
3 carrots, chopped
small bunch parsley
4 rashers streaky bacon
1.5kg 3lb boneless rolled
   shoulder or loin of veal

salt and pepper
butter
2 sprigs rosemary
2tbsp brandy
300ml ½pt veal or chicken
   stock
1tbsp flour

110

1 Lightly grease the bottom of a small roasting pan and put into it the onion, celery, carrots and parsley.
2 Cut the bacon into long thin ribbons and, using a larding needle, thread them through the meat. In the absence of a needle, make small incisions at intervals in the meat and push pieces of bacon as deeply as possible into it, using the handle of a coffee spoon.
3 Spread softened butter and rosemary leaves all over the veal, season and put in the roasting pan on top of the vegetables.
4 Heat oven to maximum, and roast the meat for half an hour or until brown on top.
5 Add the brandy to the pan, then the stock. Turn oven down to 150°C/300°F/Mark 2, and continue cooking, basting every 15 minutes or so, for two hours or until the meat is tender and the juices run out clear when the flesh is pierced.
6 Carve the meat in slices if liked, or leave to carve at the table. If carved, cover with foil to prevent drying out while making the sauce.
7 Put the roasting pan over direct heat. Stir in the flour, and add water or more stock to make up to about 450ml/¾ pint of juice. Whisk while bringing to the boil, then push through a sieve.
8 Pour the sauce round the carved slices before serving, or hand in a sauceboat if carving at table.

Grand Marnier Pancakes

Pancake batter
250g 8oz plain flour
pinch of salt
2 eggs
2 egg yolks

600ml 1pt milk or milk and
      water mixed
2tbsp oil

Crème patissière
300ml ½pt milk
2 egg yolks
50g 2oz caster sugar
20g ¾oz flour
20g ¾oz cornflour

vanilla essence
grated rind of 2 oranges
2tbsp Grand Marnier
icing sugar

1 Put all batter ingredients into liquidizer and blend until smooth. Leave to stand for half an hour and then make 16 medium sized very thin pancakes.
2 Scald the milk.
3 Cream egg yolks with sugar. Mix in the flour and cornflour. Pour on milk and mix well.
4 Return mixture to pan and bring to the boil, stirring continuously. (It will go alarmingly lumpy – just keep stirring and it will become smooth.) Allow to cool slightly then add vanilla essence, orange rind and Grand Marnier.
5 Divide mixture between pancakes. Roll each pancake up and dust heavily with icing sugar. Place under a hot grill until sugar begins to caramelize. Serve hot, cold or warm.

MENU 31

HAM AND QUAILS' EGG SALAD
COQ AU VIN BLANC
LEMON MOUSSE

Introduction
A pretty nest of salad to start with, a lighter version of the classic coq au vin, and a rich but tangy mousse. This menu needs some time and skill, but very little last-minute fuss.

Cook's gear
Perforated spoon for poaching quails' eggs.

An electric whisk for the mousse is a great help.

Cook's tips
Quails' eggs can be bought raw or cooked from 'gourmet' shops and can be ordered from specialist food shops or high class poulterers. Hens' eggs taste much the same but are not as pretty – use one hen's egg per person, poaching for 3–4 minutes.

The eggs can be added hot, warm or cold to the salad.

The fat from the hot chicken sauce can be easily lifted by laying successive sheets of absorbent paper on the surface of the liquid.

If whisking the mousse with a hand whisk, put the bowl over a saucepan of simmering water to speed things up. Once thick enough to leave a ribbon-like trail when the whisk is lifted, stand the bowl in cold water and continue whisking until cold.

Getting ahead
The spinach, lettuce and leek can be prepared the day before. Leave leek in iced water.

The coq au vin is, if anything, nicer made up to two days before.

The mousse can be made between 6 and 24 hours ahead.

Vegetable or salad?

Rice is generally served with coq au vin, but noodles, mashed potatoes or boiled new potatoes are good too. Serve with mangetout peas or small French beans.

Ham and Quails' Egg Salad

2 young leeks
250g 8oz spinach, washed
   and de-stalked
4 thin slices smoked ham
3tbsp oil

1tbsp wine vinegar
salt and black pepper
32 quails' eggs, preferably raw
2tsp chervil leaves, roughly
   chopped

1 Wash leeks and cut into 5cm/2in lengths, then finely lengthways into thinnest needleshreds. Put in iced water and leave to curl.
2 Shred spinach and ham into very fine strips.
3 Not more than an hour before dinner, drain and dry the leeks. Toss with the spinach and ham in a dressing made by combining the oil, vinegar and seasonings.
4 Divide the salad between eight plates and form careful nests with a dip in each to take four quails' eggs.
5 Break the eggs, eight at a time, onto a dinner plate, keeping them separate. Bring a frying-pan of water to the boil and slip the eggs in. Simmer for a minute, then lift out with a perforated spoon and drain on a folded cloth. Repeat until all the eggs are cooked.
6 Put four eggs in each nest and sprinkle with chervil.

Coq au Vin Blanc

50g 2oz butter
2 roasting chickens, jointed
   into 4 pieces each
plain flour
250g 8oz button onions,
   peeled
250g 8oz button mushrooms
bouquet garni: bay leaf, thyme,
   parsley, celery, tied together

1 clove garlic, crushed
450ml ¾pt flowery white
   wine (e.g. Riesling or
   Sylvaner)
450ml ¾pt chicken stock
salt and pepper
fried bread croûtons

1 Heat half the butter in a pan. Dust each chicken joint with flour and brown in the butter. Remove.

2 Add remaining butter and brown first onions and then mushrooms. Tip out excess fat.
3 Put everything – except the croûtons – into the pan, cover and simmer until tender (about 40 minutes).
4 Discard herbs and dish up chicken. If sauce is greasy skim it. If too thin boil rapidly to reduce it and then spoon over the chicken and vegetables.
5 Add croûtons at the last minute.

Lemon Mousse

6tbsp water
15g ½oz gelatine
6 eggs, separated
300g 10oz caster sugar
juice and finely grated rind of 2
    lemons

600ml 1pt double cream,
    lightly whipped
6tbsp browned chopped
    almonds

1 Put water into small saucepan. Sprinkle gelatine over surface and leave to soak for about 10 minutes.
2 Whisk egg yolks and sugar until thick, pale and mousse-like, gradually incorporating lemon juice and rind.
3 Melt gelatine over very low heat without allowing it to boil. Stir into egg and lemon mixture.
4 To speed up setting, stand the bowl in water with ice cubes. Keep stirring. As mousse begins to set, add half the cream.
5 Whisk egg whites until stiff. Fold into mixture. Pour into dish.
6 Refrigerate to set. Decorate with nuts and remaining cream.

MENU 32

AVOCADO WITH STRAWBERRY VINAIGRETTE
YOUVARLAKIA
COEURS À LA CRÈME

Introduction

The Middle-Eastern light and lemony forcemeat balls are preceded by an exceptionally pretty first course and followed by little home-made sweet cheeses – a good summer dinner.

Cook's gear

Plain white plates show off the avocado dish best.

Perforated spoon and a large shallow pan (or two frying pans) for the meat balls.

Coeurs à la crème moulds give the traditional heart-shaped cheeses but they can be made in ramekins – fill with mixture, secure muslin tightly over the top of each one with a rubber band. Turn the ramekins over, muslin down, on a stainless steel cooling rack to drain.

Cook's tips

The avocados must be perfect. Cut one open and check that they are not end-of-season ones with blackish fibres and spots in the stem end – they will discolour quickly and look unattractive.

Take trouble getting the balance of sweetness and tartness of the first course right; the strawberry flavour must be there but should not overwhelm the avocado.

Getting ahead

Make the strawberry dressing up to six hours in advance, but arrange the avocado on the plates not more than half an hour before dinner.

The meat balls can be made up to two days ahead and refrigerated. Add the egg and lemon to the sauce when reheating.

The cheeses are best made 48 hours ahead of time to allow them to lose any whey. Turn out two hours before dinner.

116

Vegetable or salad?

There is a little rice in the meat balls, but more (boiled rather than fried) is needed to mop up the sauce. Tiny carrots mixed with peas would be good too, or omit them and serve a raw spinach and chicory salad to follow.

Avocado with Strawberry Vinaigrette

300ml ½pt salad oil (not olive) sugar
250g 8oz fresh strawberries salt and pepper
lemon juice 4 avocado pears

1 Liquidize oil and strawberries.
2 Season to taste with lemon juice, sugar, salt and pepper.
3 Pour enough sauce on to each plate to cover the base.
4 Lay each peeled avocado half, flat side down, on a board. Cut evenly across into slices. 'Fan' the slices so that they form a tightly overlapping row.
5 Paint the exposed parts of the avocado with oil to delay discolouration.
6 With a fish slice lift each sliced avocado half into place on top of the strawberry sauce.

Youvarlakia

1kg 2lb minced veal sea salt and black pepper
1 onion, finely chopped chicken or veal stock for
4tbsp cooked rice poaching
6tbsp parsley, chopped 1 egg yolk
2 eggs, separated juice of 1 lemon

1 Mix veal with onion, rice, parsley, egg whites, salt and pepper.
2 Form into oval shapes, the size of plums. Arrange in layers in buttered sauté pan.
3 Add enough stock to cover. Simmer for 40 minutes, topping up with water if liquid reduces to less than approximately 450ml/ ¾ pint. Lift onto serving dish with a perforated spoon.
4 Mix the three yolks with lemon juice. Reheat cooking liquid and add a ladleful to yolks. Pour back into saucepan. Stir over a low heat, without allowing it to boil, until thickened. Check seasoning and pour over meat.

Coeurs à la Crème

500g	1lb	cottage cheese	600ml	1pt	double cream
100g	4oz	icing sugar	4		egg whites

To serve

300ml	½pt	single cream	250g	8oz	fresh raspberries, grapes or cherries

1 First day: push cheese through a sieve. Mix in sugar and double cream.
2 Whisk egg whites until stiff. Fold into cheese mixture.
3 Fill coeur à la crème moulds with the mixture, or use ramekins as described under Cook's Tips. Drain in cool place for two days.
4 To serve, turn out on to individual plates. Pour over single cream. Serve with a few fresh summer fruits.

MENU 33

POPPY SEED PEARS
VEAL À LA FLORENTINE
BEST RICE PUDDING

Introduction
In spite of the cost of veal this is not a wildly expensive dinner; you only need 100g/4oz of veal per person to produce a most luxurious dish. The rice pudding is light, creamy, and nothing to do with school dinners.

Cook's gear
Melon baller for extracting pear cores and a piping bag with a plain nozzle for filling the pears.

Cook's tips
If the butcher has not sliced the veal thinly and evenly, put each slice between two sheets of poly-wrap and beat with a rolling pin to spread and flatten them.

To loosen tomato skins, dip them in boiling water for five seconds.

Getting ahead
The pears discolour slightly after slicing, so fill them 4–6 hours in advance and chill to firm the filling. Slice them not more than half an hour before dinner.

The veal is reheatable. Ideally make any time up to 12 hours ahead.

The rice pudding can be completed the day before and perhaps given a final thin jam glaze a few hours before dinner, to ensure a fresh shine.

Vegetable or salad?
Noodles would be nicest – say a mixture of green and white tagliatelli. Perhaps follow with a plain butterhead lettuce salad dressed with walnut oil and lemon juice.

Poppy Seed Pears

250g 8oz Stilton cheese
250g 8oz cream cheese
8 ripe dessert pears, washed
but not peeled

squeeze of lemon juice
2 bunches watercress

Dressing
3tbsp oil
1tbsp lemon juice

2tbsp poppy seeds
salt and freshly ground pepper

1 Beat together Stilton and cream cheese. Spoon into piping bag fitted with plain nozzle.
2 Using a melon baller, remove centres of pears. Sprinkle channel with lemon juice and pipe with cheese mixture. Refrigerate until ready to serve (at least two hours).
3 Put dressing ingredients into screw-top jar. Shake well. Check seasoning.
4 Slice each pear across into thin round slices. Arrange in concentric circles on a serving plate. Spoon over dressing and garnish with watercress.

Veal à la Florentine

175g 6oz butter	salt, pepper and nutmeg
8 veal escalopes, beaten thin	50g 2oz flour
1 clove garlic, crushed	850ml 1½pt milk
6 tomatoes, peeled and sliced	175g 6oz cheese
750g 1½lb spinach	2tbsp breadcrumbs

1 Melt 50g/2oz butter in a frying pan. Brown veal on both sides. Remove to a plate. Cut into thin strips.
2 Fry garlic in a little more butter for few seconds. Add tomatoes and fry briefly without allowing to break up.
3 Line pie dish with slices of tomato and add the veal strips.
4 Wash spinach and strip off stalks.
5 Cook in boiling water until soft but still bright green (2–3 minutes).
6 Squeeze all moisture from spinach and chop roughly.
7 Return to saucepan. Coat well with 50g/2oz of remaining butter and season with salt, pepper and nutmeg. Spread over veal in pie dish.
8 Set oven to 220°C/425°F/Mark 7.
9 For the sauce: melt remaining butter and stir in flour. Cook for few minutes. Add milk. Stir until boiling. Remove from heat. Add three-quarters of the cheese, mix and pour sauce over spinach.
10 Mix remaining cheese with breadcrumbs and sprinkle over the sauce. Bake until brown – about 10 minutes.

Best Rice Pudding

1 small fresh pineapple	3tbsp smooth apricot jam
2tbsp kirsch	2 egg whites
sugar	300ml ½pt double cream

For the rice cream

1 litre 2pt milk	50g 2oz butter
100g 4oz pudding rice	50g 2oz sugar

1 Set oven to 150°C/300°F/Mark 2.
2 Mix rice cream ingredients together in heavy saucepan and simmer gently until rice is soft and the milk is absorbed (about 60 minutes). Stir in final stages to prevent burning.

3 Cut top off pineapple and keep for decoration. Skin and thinly slice the fruit.
4 Put slices in bowl with kirsch and sprinkle with sugar. Cover tightly and refrigerate for about six hours. Pour juices into a saucepan and add the jam.
5 Stir over a low heat until jam has melted. Boil to a thick syrup. Allow to cool to tepid.
6 Tip cold rice pudding into a large bowl. Beat until smooth. Whip egg whites and cream separately until stiff. Fold them together and then into rice to produce creamy but just-solid consistency.
7 Shape mixture into an oval mound on a flat dish/plate. Using the handle of a teaspoon, mark a lattice pattern of grooves over the top to resemble a pineapple skin. Chill in freezer for 10 minutes.
8 Cut the leafy pineapple top in half. Wash one half (discard the other) and place it at head of rice 'pineapple'.
9 Carefully spoon the just-liquid apricot glaze all over the pudding so that it runs into the grooves.
10 Serve the chilled pineapple slices separately.

MENU 34

MELON WITH GINGER WINE
POULET AU RIZ
LEMON MERINGUE PIE

Introduction

Melon, chicken and rice, lemon meringue pie – it could be a pretty ordinary dinner, but if the melons are perfect and soused in ginger wine, the chicken is creamy and rich and the pie has the tartness of real lemon curd and slightly toffee meringue, what could be better?

Cook's gear

Large bowl for rapid cooling of chicken – see below.

Cook's tips

The melons should be soft at the end opposite the stalk and they should smell headily fragrant.

Cool the boiled chicken in the stock to prevent the flesh drying out – set the saucepan in a bowl of water in the sink with the tap dripping steadily into the bowl, cooling the water. The chickens will cool more rapidly, and more safely, than if left at room temperature.

Getting ahead

The melons can be split, de-seeded and covered in poly-wrap to chill (unwrapped they will spoil the taste of milk and butter in the refrigerator).

The chicken dish can be made the day before and reheated. Keep refrigerated.

The pie can be made up to two days before but do not add the meringue – it 'weeps' if made more than four hours in advance. If it must be done in advance put the whole pie, with unbaked meringue, in the freezer. Bake from frozen.

Vegetable or salad?

Small whole courgettes (if possible with their flowers still attached), briefly boiled and lightly buttered. Or use them raw and finely sliced as a salad in a light dressing.

Melon with Ginger Wine

4 large or 8 small Ogen or   ginger wine
   Charentais melons

1   If melons are large, cut in half across the equator, if small cut off stalk end.
2   Scoop out seeds.
3   Steady each melon or melon-half by slicing a thin piece from each base.
4   Fill the melons with ginger wine. Chill.

Poulet au Riz

1 litre 2pt water   85g   3oz butter
2 chicken stock cubes   50g   2oz flour
sprig of thyme, leaf of a leek,   6tbsp cream
   stick of celery, slice of onion   salt and pepper
2 chickens, not trussed and
   with fat near tail removed

To serve
boiled rice

1   Put water in saucepan large enough to hold chickens. Bring to boil with stock cubes and seasonings. Add the chickens and simmer until tender.
2   Cool birds in the stock as quickly as possible.
3   When chicken is lukewarm or cool enough to handle, remove skin, gristle and bones and cut flesh into reasonable sized pieces. Cover the chicken with foil or poly-wrap to prevent flesh from drying out while the sauce is being made.
4   Strain stock and let it settle. Skim off fat or use successive sheets of absorbent paper laid across surface to lift off the grease.
5   Melt the butter and add the flour. Stir for a minute and then add the stock, stirring until it comes to the boil.

6   Boil fast to reduce the sauce to a syrupy, thick and shiny consistency – thicker than you will eventually want it because the cream will thin it down.
7   Add chicken to the sauce. Stir in the cream and season with salt and pepper as needed. Reheat briefly and tip onto a bed of hot boiled rice.

Lemon Meringue Pie

350g 12oz plain flour
pinch of salt
2tsp caster sugar

250g 8oz butter
2   egg yolks
very cold water

For the filling
50g 2oz cornflour
600ml 1pt milk
50g 2oz sugar

4   egg yolks
grated rind and juice of 2 lemons

For the meringue
4   egg whites

250g 8oz caster sugar and a little extra to sprinkle over top of pile

1   Make pastry: sift flour with salt and sugar. Rub in the butter.
2   Mix egg yolks with four tablespoons of the ice-cold water. Add to flour and butter mixture. Lightly work into a dough.
3   Roll out pastry and line 30cm/12in flan ring. Chill.
4   Set oven to 190°C/375°F/Mark 5.
5   Bake pastry blind (lined with paper and filled with dried beans, pebbles or pennies to prevent bubbling up) until cooked, 25–35 minutes.
6   Mix cornflour with tablespoon of milk. Heat remaining milk. Pour this onto cornflour, stir well and then return mixture to pan. Boil for 3–4 minutes stirring continuously. Add sugar.
7   Allow to cool slightly. Beat in egg yolks, lemon juice and rind. Pour into pastry case and bake for 2–5 minutes to set the lemon filling.
8   Whisk egg whites until stiff. Add half the sugar and continue whisking until very stiff and shiny.
9   Fold in remaining sugar. Pile meringue onto pie, covering all the lemon filling. Dust with a little extra caster sugar. Bake for five minutes or until meringue is pale brown.

MENU 35

CUCUMBER WITH YOGHURT AND MINT
MARMALADE DUCK
CHOCOLATE-COATED ICE CREAM

Introduction

Marmalade duck is a less sweet version of the more usual canard à l'orange. The ice cream balls are given a crackly chocolate coating – rather a fiddle to do but amusing and pretty to look at.

Cook's gear

Ice cream scoop.

A sorbetière or ice cream maker is not essential, but the freezer must be efficient – the ice-making compartment of a refrigerator is no good.

Cook's tips

For yoghurt-haters, substitute soured cream for a richer but still refreshing cucumber salad dressing.

Bitter 'Oxford' marmalade is the best. If unavoidable use sweet orange marmalade and add a teaspoon of black treacle.

To skim fat from stock or sauce, lay successive sheets of absorbent kitchen paper on the surface – the paper will lift the fat.

Use home made ice cream or *non* 'soft-scoop' which is too soft to handle. Use good quality, not 'cake icing' chocolate.

To speed up freezing of ice cream and sorbets, have all whisks, bowls etc. well chilled before use.

If using a food processor for re-whisking, the mixture can be frozen rock-solid and simply broken into chunks and processed to smooth creaminess. Refreeze.

Getting ahead

The cucumber can be prepared up to 24 hours in advance, but is best done on the morning of the dinner. Add the dressing two hours before serving.

126

The stock from the giblets, and the sauce (paragraphs 6 and 7) can be made the day before. Do not forget to add the de-fatted roasting juices to the sauce after roasting the ducks. The ducks can be roasted in the afternoon of the dinner, and will retain their fresh flavour if reheated – this would not be so if they were cooked the day before.

The ice cream should be dipped at least six hours before serving, and can be done a week in advance.

Vegetable or salad?
Small minted new potatoes would be suitable, and perhaps a watercress and orange salad served with, rather than after, the duck.

Cucumber with Yoghurt and Mint

2 cucumbers
4tbsp oil
1tbsp red wine vinegar
2tbsp finely chopped fresh
  mint
½tsp sugar
salt and black pepper
300ml ½pt plain yoghurt
1 clove garlic, crushed
mint leaves for decoration

1 Peel cucumber. Slice very thinly. Soak the slices in salty water for half an hour.
2 Mix together oil, vinegar, mint, sugar and pepper.
3 Rinse cucumber and dry on absorbent paper. Toss in dressing. Divide between eight small plates.
4 Add garlic to yoghurt. Season with pepper, and with salt if needed. Put spoonful of yoghurt on top of each cucumber portion. Decorate with mint leaf. Chill.

Marmalade Duck

2 × 3kg/6lb or 3 × 2.25kg/4½lb
  ducklings
4tbsp soy sauce
4tbsp marmalade
4 shallots, finely chopped
30g 1oz butter
the ducks' livers
4tbsp orange juice
300ml ½pt stock made from
  giblets (except livers)
2tsp cornflour
salt and pepper

1 Set oven to 220°C/425°F/Mark 7.
2 Prick ducks all over with fork or skewer. Rub inside and out with salt. Place on a rack over a roasting tin.

3   Roast for one hour, turning once during cooking.
4   Skim fat from pan juices. Tip any juices from inside ducks into pan.
5   Brush skin with half of the soy sauce and marmalade. Return to oven for 30–60 minutes until browned and tender.
6   Meanwhile, fry shallots in butter until soft and pale brown. Add chopped duck liver. Fry for two minutes. Add orange juice, remaining soy sauce and marmalade.
7   Mix a tablespoon of stock with cornflour. Add rest of stock, mix thoroughly. Add to pan with liver. Bring to boil, stirring. Simmer until of syrupy consistency. Season with salt and pepper.
8   Place ducks on serving dish. Add any juices to sauce, reheat and hand separately.

Chocolate Coated Ice Cream

600ml   1pt milk
300ml   ½pt cream
250g   8oz caster sugar
8 egg yolks

100g   4oz good quality dark chocolate
2tbsp tasteless vegetable oil (e.g. peanut or corn oil)

1   Set freezer to coldest.
2   Put milk, cream and sugar into a heavy saucepan. Slowly bring to boil.
3   Beat yolks in a large bowl. Pour boiling milky mixture onto them, whisking.
4   Strain into ice trays. Cool. Freeze until edges are solid but middle is still fairly soft.
5   Tip into chilled bowl. Whisk until smooth, pale and creamy. Refreeze.
6   Shape the ice cream into balls, and freeze them on an open tray until very hard.
7   Melt chocolate with oil over very low heat, stirring until smooth. Cool.
8   Dip each ball into the chocolate using spoons to turn and coat them all over as quickly as possible. Place on oiled trays and refreeze. Remove from freezer half an hour before serving to allow them to soften slightly.

MENU 36

*CHERRY TOMATO AND
SCAMPI SALAD
SWEETBREADS IN CREAM AND
CALVADOS
BLACKCURRANT LEAF SORBET*

Introduction
The main dish of this menu, the sweetbreads, needs time to prepare, but can be quite easily mastered. The prawn and tomato salad starter is astringent and light and the blackcurrant leaf ice is subtle-flavoured and curiously good.

Cook's gear
A sorbetière or ice cream maker is not essential, but the freezer must be efficient – the ice-making compartment of a refrigerator is no good.

Cook's tips
If tiny cherry tomatoes are unavailable use any sweet ripe tomato and slice them horizontally – not stem to stern.

The secret of delicate sweetbreads is making sure all traces of blood are washed away before cooking.

Scented geranium leaves, strongly scented rose petals, ripe rose-hips, or China tea all make unusual sorbets. Treat fresh things exactly as the blackcurrant leaves, but add the China tea (2 heaped table-spoons) to the boiling syrup *after* it is removed from the heat.

To speed up freezing of the sorbet, have all whisks, bowls etc. well chilled before use.

If using a food processor for re-whisking, the mixture can be frozen rock-solid and simply broken into chunks and processed to smooth creaminess. Refreeze.

Getting ahead
The salad is best prepared 4–12 hours before serving.

The sweetbreads can be cooked the day before. Add the cream and lemon juice only on re-heating.

130

The sorbet is best made between 1 and 4 days ahead of time.

Chill serving glasses before use and have the sorbet scooped into balls and stored on foil-covered trays ready for last minute serving.

Vegetable or salad?

The sweetbreads need a bed of steamed or boiled rice, and some mild, slightly crisp vegetable would be good too – say shredded Chinese leaves, boiled for three minutes then drained and buttered.

Cherry Tomato and Scampi Salad

2tbsp olive oil
4 shallots, finely chopped
1 clove garlic, finely chopped
350g 12oz button
　mushrooms, finely sliced
500g 1lb raw scampi (frozen
　is fine)

1tbsp tomato purée
1tsp sugar
1tbsp marjoram, chopped
500g 1lb 'cherry' tomatoes
salt and pepper
fresh basil, chopped

1　Heat oil. Cook shallots over low heat until soft. Add garlic.
2　Turn up heat, fry mushrooms for two minutes. Add scampi, tomato purée, sugar and marjoram. Simmer for one minute until the scampi are just firm. Allow to cool.
3　Dip tomatoes into boiling water for 4–5 seconds until skin peels off easily. Halve if on the large side.
4　Mix with scampi mixture. Check seasoning. Tip into serving dish. Chill. Scatter with basil just before serving.

Sweetbreads in Cream and Calvados

1kg 2lb sweetbreads
300ml ½pt wine
1 chicken stock cube
50g 2oz butter
1 medium onion, chopped
2 apples, peeled and chopped
250g 8oz mushrooms, sliced

2tbsp calvados
40g 1½oz flour
200ml ⅓pt double cream
juice of 1 lemon
salt and pepper
500g 1lb long grain rice,
　cooked

1　Soak sweetbreads in successive changes of cold water for two or three hours or until the water no longer turns pink.

2 Transfer to saucepan, cover with boiling water (about 600ml/1pt) and wine. Simmer for six minutes. Drain, reserving liquid.
3 When cool enough remove membrane and sinewy parts. Cover sweetbreads to prevent drying out, and put to one side.
4 Remove any scum from the cooking liquid and bring to boil with chicken stock cube. Boil rapidly until reduced to 450ml/¾ pint.
5 Melt butter in frying pan and gently cook onion until soft. Add apple, fry until lightly browned. Remove with perforated spoon.
6 Using the same pan, fry sweetbreads, adding more butter if necessary. They should brown slightly all over. Take care not to break them up by stirring too much.
7 Add sliced mushrooms. Fry for further two minutes. Add calvados and, standing back, set a match to the pan. When flames have died down stir in flour.
8 Add stock. Stir until it starts to simmer. Cover and simmer very gently for 15 minutes.
9 Strain liquid and return it to pan. Boil rapidly until thick and syrupy.
10 Add cream and lemon juice. Check seasoning.
11 Serve sweetbreads and mushrooms on bed of rice. Heat onion and apple mixture and spoon over top. Coat with the cream sauce.

Blackcurrant Leaf Sorbet

about 60 blackcurrant leaves
1 litre   2pt   water
350g   12oz   pale runny honey

thinly pared rind and juice of 4 large lemons

1 Set freezer to coldest.
2 Boil everything together for five minutes.
3 Allow to cool. Strain.
4 Freeze until edges are solid but centre is still soft. Whisk until smooth. Return to freezer. Keep whisking at intervals until smooth and creamy. If mixture is too hard to scoop, remove to the refrigerator for half an hour before serving.

MENU 37

KIPPER FILLET SALAD
VEAL SAUSAGES
COFFEE SOUFFLÉ

Introduction
This dinner is the gastronome's sausage and mash, followed by a deliciously creamy cold soufflé.

Cook's gear
Sausage casings can be bought but are not strictly necessary.
A 15cm/6in soufflé dish with a double band of greaseproof paper tied round the top so that it sticks up 2.5cm/1in all round the rim.

Cook's tips
Frozen kipper fillets are wonderfully easy to skin when half thawed.
If whisking the mousse with a hand whisk, put the bowl over a saucepan of simmering water to speed things up. Once thick enough to leave a ribbon-like trail when the whisk is lifted, stand the bowl in cold water and continue whisking until cold.

Getting ahead
The kipper fillets must be marinated for at least six hours and can be done with advantage 48 hours in advance.
The sausages can be prepared in advance but are best cooked not more than two hours ahead of time.
The soufflé can be made the day before but leave the band of greaseproof paper in place until decorating, which should not be done much more than four hours before dinner.

Vegetable or salad?
Mashed potatoes are a must with the sausages. Follow with a slightly bitter salad – say endive, chicory and watercress.

133

Kipper Fillet Salad

500g 1lb frozen kipper fillets
8tbsp oil
juice of 1 lemon

1 large onion, finely sliced
1 bay leaf
freshly ground black pepper

To serve
hot French bread

1 Skin fillets when half thawed. Cut into strips if very large. Allow to thaw completely and then put them in a deep dish.
2 Add other ingredients, coating fillets well. Cover dish with poly-wrap and refrigerate for 2–3 days.
3 Serve with hot French bread.

Veal Sausages

For the sausages
750g 1½lb pie veal
750g 1½lb pork belly
6tbsp breadcrumbs
3tbsp double cream

1tbsp chopped fresh chervil
salt and pepper

For the sauce
50g 2oz butter
1 onion, chopped
2 dessert apples, peeled and sliced
30g 1oz flour
1tbsp sherry

450ml ¾pt veal or chicken stock
1tsp pale French mustard
salt and pepper
6tbsp double cream

1 Mince together (or blend in a processor) the sausage ingredients. Shape into sausages and fry slowly in very little oil to brown gently and evenly. When firm lift out onto serving dish and keep warm.
2 To make the sauce: tip excess pork fat out of frying pan. Melt butter and in it soften the onion.
3 Fry the apple slices until soft and evenly brown. Lift out and place on top of sausages.
4 Add flour to the pan, stir for a few seconds and then add the sherry, stock, mustard, salt and pepper. Bring to the boil stirring. Add the cream and boil until of syrupy consistency. Pour over sausages.

Coffee Soufflé

175ml 6fl oz strong black
  coffee (use 3tsp instant)
15g ½oz powdered gelatine
6 eggs, separated
175g 6oz caster sugar

2tbsp rum
300ml ½pt double cream,
  lightly whipped
30g 1oz grated chocolate

1   Put coffee into small saucepan. Sprinkle gelatine over surface and leave to soak for about 10 minutes.
2   Whisk egg yolks and sugar until thick, pale and mousse-like, gradually incorporating rum.
3   Melt gelatine over very low heat without allowing it to boil. Stir into egg and sugar mixture.
4   To speed up setting, stand the bowl in water with ice cubes. Keep stirring and, as mousse begins to set, fold in the cream.
5   Whisk egg whites until stiff. Fold into mixture. Pour into soufflé dish.
6   Refrigerate to set. Remove the band of paper. Decorate with the chocolate, pressing it round the protruding rim and sprinkling it evenly over top.

MENU 38

SMOKED TROUT AND CUCUMBER PÂTÉ
ROAST TURKEY BREAST
GREEK FRUIT SALAD

Introduction
The smoked trout pâté looks spectacular in a fish shape with cucumber scales, and is fun (but fiddly) to do. By contrast the roast turkey breast is as easy, easier, than pie and the Greek fruit salad is both easy and startlingly pretty.

Cook's gear
An electric mixer is useful for extracting tiny smoked trout bones: whisk the flaked flesh in the bowl – the small bones stick to the wire whisk.

Alternatively mince or sieve the flesh to extract the bones.

Thin string and muslin or J-cloth for turkey breast.

Finger bowls and cloth napkins for fruit.

Cook's tips
For small elegant individual helpings of the pâté, forget the cucumber and wrap a spoon of the pâté carefully in a slice of smoked salmon, like a parcel, and lay one on each plate.

Paint all over with salad oil for a shine and add a few leaves of mâche (lamb's lettuce) or watercress for colour.

Serve with toast.

To make the turkey roast 'self-basting' and to avoid tedious tying up with string, brush the breast, stuffed but not tied, with melted butter, then roll it up tightly in muslin or a pre-boiled J-cloth. Paint all over with more melted butter.

The butter will baste the turkey, which will brown through the cloth.

Ice for the fruit can be crushed in a food processor. Or put cubes in a strong polythene bag, wrap in a cloth and crush with a rolling pin.

136

Getting ahead

The trout mixture can be made up to 24 hours ahead but should not be completed or decorated until about 4 hours before dinner.

The turkey breast can be prepared for the oven the day before and kept refrigerated, but it is vital that the stuffing is chilled when put into the meat.

The Greek fruit salad can be half-prepared in advance. Fruit that will not discolour can be cut up etc., but pears, apples and bananas should be chilled in their skins, and only cut up shortly before dinner. Discoloration can be retarded by brushing the cut surfaces with lemon juice and keeping the fruit well chilled.

Vegetable or salad?

The turkey breast is fairly plain, so luxurious sliced potato baked with cream, crushed garlic, salt and pepper would be wonderful. Or you might serve rice and a dish of ratatouille (cut up courgettes, aubergines, skinned tomatoes flavoured with garlic and stewed slowly in oil to a soft mass).

Smoked Trout and Cucumber Pâté

1 cucumber
4 large smoked trout
450ml ¾pt double cream
lemon juice

1tbsp creamed horseradish
salt and pepper
salad oil

1 Peel the cucumber, but keep the skins. Finely slice the flesh.
2 Cover cucumber slices with well-salted water and leave for half an hour.
3 Skin, flake and carefully bone fish.
4 Whip cream until thick. Stir into trout. Season with lemon juice, horseradish, salt and pepper.
5 Form pâté into shape of a fish on a large flat plate.
6 Drain and rinse cucumber. Pat dry with absorbent paper. Arrange over pâté to imitate fish scales. Use some of the cucumber skin to represent tail and gills, and a round piece for the eye.
7 Brush lightly with oil.

Roast Turkey Breast

1.5kg 3lb turkey breast
100g 4oz cooked ham, diced
2 hardboiled eggs, finely
  chopped
100g 4oz green or black
  olives, finely chopped
100g 4oz cooked rice
salt and pepper
bacon rashers or melted butter

1 Set oven to 200°C/400°F/Mark 6.
2 Split turkey breast horizontally from the thick side towards the thin side without cutting it quite in two.
3 Open out and put between two sheets of poly-wrap. Flatten it with a rolling pin until very much larger, and one inch thick all over.
4 Mix eggs, olives, rice and seasoning together and spread over turkey. Roll up and tie with string.
5 Cover with strips of bacon or brush with melted butter. Roast for about one hour. Serve with pan juices.

Greek Fruit Salad

assortment of fruit – anything
  available to provide variety
  of colour, flavour and texture
crushed ice

1 Wipe or wash fruit as for fruit salad but cut into chunks or sticks large enough to eat with fingers. (Leave whole until serving any fruit likely to discolour.)
2 Arrange in clumps on a large deep platter or on individual dinner plates. Cover with poly-wrap and chill.
3 Tip crushed ice or small ice cubes all over the fruit just before serving. It is eaten with the fingers.

MENU 39

AMERICAN SPINACH SALAD
BOEUF À LA BOURGUIGNONNE
LINZER TORTE

Introduction

A good rich stew is a rare treat these days. The light spinach starter should leave plenty of room for it, but the torte is rich, so go easy on the portion sizes.

Cook's gear

A deep flan ring or, better still, loose-bottomed flan tin for the torte.

Cook's tips

If the salad is to be served in a less rich menu, or as a lunch-time main course, a spoon or two of soured cream in the dressing is good.

The secrets of a good rich stew are assiduous removal of fat and gristle before cooking and careful, thorough, browning of the meat and vegetables before adding the liquid.

The least messy way to cope with the pastry is to tip it, crumbly bits and all, into the flan ring and press it to cover the bottom and sides with knuckles and fingers. Rolling out with a pin is very tricky.

Getting ahead

Prepare everything for the salad but do not add dressing until just before dinner. Keep spinach in a plastic bag in the refrigerator.

Make the stew up to three days ahead. Keep refrigerated.

The torte is best made on the day of the dinner but can be made up to three days ahead. Serve tepid, not chilled or hot.

Vegetable or salad

The beef needs rice, noodles, or mashed potatoes to mop up the sauce. One green vegetable, say broad beans, would be good. Add them raw to the stew, for colour and ease of serving, when the stew is reheated.

American Spinach Salad

750g 1½lb very young tender spinach leaves	2tbsp olive oil
8–10 large rashers streaky bacon	2tbsp salad oil
100g 4oz walnut halves	1tbsp red wine vinegar
	1 clove garlic, crushed
	salt and pepper

1 Destalk, wash and roughly chop spinach. Dry well.
2 Cut rind from bacon. Grill or fry bacon and rind until crisp.
3 Grind the rind or chop very finely.
4 Roughly chop bacon.
5 Put spinach, bacon rind, bacon and walnuts in a bowl.
6 Mix remaining ingredients for dressing.
7 Just before serving, toss salad in dressing. Serve in individual bowls.

Boeuf à la Bourguignonne

2kg 4lb piece lean stewing beef	30g 1oz flour
oil for frying meat	450ml ¾pt beef stock
450ml ¾pt red wine	bouquet garni: stick of celery, bayleaf, parsley, thyme – tied together with string
15 small onions/shallots, peeled	salt and pepper
50g 2oz butter	
350g 12oz flat mushrooms, sliced	

1 Cut beef in thick steaks.
2 Brown each steak fast in very hot oil.
3 As each steak is browned lay it in a flame-proof casserole.
4 Swish pan with some of the wine, loosening any sediment. Pour over meat.
5 Fry onions in butter until an even brown.
6 Add mushrooms. Cook for few minutes.
7 Stir in flour. Add rest of wine and stock. Bring to boil, stirring.
8 Pour over steaks. Add bouquet garni, salt and pepper. Simmer gently for 2–3 hours or until meat is tender but still in whole slices. Lift beef onto serving dish.
9 If the sauce is thin, boil fast until reduced to thick syrupy consistency. Remove bouquet garni. Pour sauce over meat.

Linzer Torte

100g	4oz	ground almonds
250g	8oz	self-raising flour
85g	3oz	icing sugar
½tsp		cinnamon
100g	4oz	soft butter
2		egg yolks

2tsp		rum
100g	4oz	raspberry jam or blackcurrant jelly
100g	4oz	sweetened apple purée

To serve
whipped cream

1 Set oven to 190°C/375°F/Mark 5.
2 Gently combine nuts with flour, 50g/2oz of the sugar, cinnamon and butter.
3 Mix egg yolks with rum. Stir into nut mixture to produce a soft dough. Work with hands if dough will not bind together, chill if dough is too sticky.
4 Line 20cm/8in flan ring with two-thirds of the pastry, pressing it up sides and patching any cracks.
5 Mix all but two tablespoons of jam or jelly with the apple. Use to fill flan.
6 Roll out remaining pastry. Cut into strips. Lay across flan to form lattice top.
7 Bake for 30 minutes or until pastry is cooked and browned.
8 Remove from oven and while hot fill spaces between lattice with jam or jelly. It will melt to fill gaps evenly.
9 When cold, dust with the remaining icing sugar. Serve with cream.

MENU 40

CEVICHE
DINNER PARTY MEATBALLS
BAKED LEMON PUDDING

Introduction

Ceviche is a Mexican raw fish salad with avocado. The most conservative Englishman would not know the fish is raw, however — it is 'cooked' to tender whiteness by marinating in lime or lemon juice. The meatballs are meaty and rich, but need not be clumsy, and the baked lemon pudding is the most elegant version of a classic English pudding.

Cook's gear

A lemon grater with a very fine (as for nutmeg) gauge for the lemon rind. Coarse graters include the pith, which is bitter.

Cook's tips

The smaller you cut the fish the quicker it will 'cook' in the lime juice. Avoid brown or greyish bits of fish, and make sure there is no skin or sinew. The fish must, of course, be very fresh.

Make small meatballs — they are substantial, and two or three ping-pong sized balls look better than one huge one on the plate.

Cream may be sinful with the pudding, but it is very very good. Whip it until it will just hold its shape and chill well.

Getting ahead

The fish must be marinated at least a few hours ahead of time. Between 4 and 24 hours, not more, would be fine. Add the avocado up to two hours before serving. Keep chilled until the last minute.

The meatballs can be made up to four days in advance, and kept refrigerated. Or they can be frozen — the sauce will need re-boiling to regain its consistency, however.

The lemon pudding can be made the day before. Re-heat slightly before serving — it needs to be just warm.

Vegetable or salad?

Some farinaceous dish is needed to soak up the meatball gravy. Rice is usual, but mashed potatoes or large pasta (shells or spirals) serve as well. A vegetable, such as fennel, broccoli or spring cabbage, goes well with the sweetish tomato sauce.

Ceviche

1kg   2lb fillet of monkfish or halibut, skinned and cut into thin strips
3 onions, chopped
juice of 3 lemons or 6 limes
3tbsp olive oil
cayenne pepper

2 fresh chillies, seeded and in strips (optional)
4 tomatoes, peeled and chopped
1 green pepper, seeded and chopped
2 avocado pears, peeled and diced
salt and black pepper

1   Mix together the first five ingredients. Refrigerate for about six hours, or until fish has become opaque and looks 'cooked'.
2   Add remaining ingredients, seasoning with salt and pepper just before serving.

Dinner Party Meatballs

For the meatballs
750g   1½lb minced pork
750g   1½lb minced stewing beef
1tbsp chopped fresh basil

2tbsp chopped parsley
salt and pepper
1 egg
6tbsp fresh white breadcrumbs

For the sauce
2tbsp oil, bacon fat or dripping
2 onions, sliced
1 green pepper, seeded, sliced
1 clove garlic, crushed

2tsp tomato paste
1 large can tomato soup
1tbsp sherry
salt and pepper

For the top
150ml · ¼pt soured cream

more chopped basil

1   Mix the meatball ingredients together and roll into small balls.
2   Heat the fat and fry the balls a few at a time to brown them all

143

over. Keep them rolling about in the pan to colour evenly.
3   When brown and firm to the touch lift them into a roasting tin that allows them to lie in a single layer without excessive space.
4   Set oven to 150°C/300°F/Mark 3.
5   Pour off all but a tablespoon of the fat left in the frying pan. Add the onions and sliced pepper to the pan and fry slowly until very soft. Add the rest of the sauce ingredients and mix well, loosening any stuck sediment on the pan bottom. Pour over the meatballs.
6   Bake uncovered for about 45 minutes. Lift meatballs into a warm serving dish.
7   Skim the sauce if it is excessively fatty, then mix it well and pour over the meat. Add soured cream in swirls and scatter the basil on top.

Lemon Pudding

4 lemons
100g 4oz unsalted butter
100g 4oz caster sugar
50g 2oz flour

200ml ⅓pt milk
5 eggs, separated
2 extra egg whites

To serve
whipped cream

1   Butter and dust out with sugar a large charlotte mould, large deep cake tin or soufflé dish.
2   Set oven to 180°C/350°F/Mark 4.
3   Finely grate rind of two lemons and squeeze the juice from all of them.
4   Mix the butter, sugar and flour together in a saucepan. Add the milk and stir over heat to a thick paste.
5   Beat in the lemon juice and rind, and stir over heat until the mixture leaves the sides of the pan.
6   Cool slightly and beat in the egg yolks.
7   Whisk the seven egg whites until stiff, and fold into the lemon and yolk mixture.
8   Pour into the mould, and set it in a roasting tin of boiling water.
9   Bake for an hour. The pudding will be risen, brown and set. Allow to cool and sink (about 10 minutes) then loosen the sides with a knife and turn the pudding out onto a plate. Serve lukewarm with whipped cream.

144

MENU 41

ALMOND SOUP
MELON-SHAPED LAMB ROAST
STRAWBERRY RING

Introduction

This almond soup is unusual and surprisingly light and good. The lamb is a glorified stuffed lamb shoulder, and the strawberry ring is impressively pretty – a menu with a fair bit of work in advance, but an easy ride at serving-up time.

Cook's gear

A liquidizer or coffee grinder for nuts to make the soup.

A barding or upholstery needle and strong thin string to sew up the lamb.

A piping bag and fluted nozzle for the strawberry ring (optional).

Cook's tips

Do not over-grind the almonds for the soup or they will become oily.

Use a breadknife to split the choux ring.

Getting ahead

Make the soup up to two days ahead. Keep refrigerated. Add yolks and cream on re-heating. Do not boil.

Stuff and prepare the lamb the day before but do not roast until a couple of hours before dinner. If preparing it in advance, make sure both stuffing and raw lamb are chilled before putting the two together, then keep refrigerated.

Make the choux ring well in advance and freeze. If making the day before, wrap and keep chilled – choux stales quickly. Fill and ice about four hours before dinner.

Vegetable or salad?

Pommes parisiennes (balls of potato scooped from large peeled potatoes with a melon baller, washed, dried, and cooked in a covered frying pan with clarified butter until brown and tender – you need to shake the pan frequently to stop sticking) are the best, but take time and trouble, and cannot be done more than an hour or two in advance. Sauté potatoes (boiled in their skins, peeled, sliced and fried slowly in butter with a sprig of rosemary until golden on both sides) are easier to manage. Reheat either type of potato in the oven under the lamb. For a green vegetable try finely shredded spring cabbage with a few caraway seeds, or whole mangetout peas, or a purée of peas filled into half tomàtoes and baked for 15 minutes.

Almond Soup

30g 1oz butter	pinch of cloves
1 onion, chopped	250g 8oz almonds, blanched
30g 1oz flour	300ml ½pt double cream
1 litre 2pt chicken stock	4 egg yolks
blade of mace	

1   Melt butter. Add onion and cook until soft.
2   Stir in flour. Add stock, mace and cloves. Stir until boiling. Simmer for 10 minutes. Strain into a jug.
3   Grind almonds. Mix with two tablespoons of the cream in a large bowl.
4   Blend a spoonful of strained stock with the almond mixture. Slowly incorporate remaining stock, mixing until smooth. Check seasoning. Return to pan.
5   Mix egg yolks with rest of cream. Add spoonful of warm soup to egg yolk mixture and then tip back into soup.
6   Stir well while reheating. Do not allow soup to get near to boiling point, or it will curdle.

Melon-Shaped Lamb Roast

1 boned shoulder lamb	300ml ½pt water or stock
butter	salt and pepper
sprig of rosemary	

For the stuffing
2tbsp parsley, chopped	1tsp marjoram, chopped
85g 3oz green bacon, chopped	salt and pepper

1 Mix stuffing ingredients together and push into the lamb.
2 If the butcher has left an overwide hole where he extracted the bone, or if he has split the whole shoulder, sew it up with string.
3 Using a piece of string about 4 metres/12 feet long, tie the shoulder so that the indentations made by the string resemble the grooves in a melon or the lines between segments of a beachball. To do this, tie the string firmly round the shoulder once, making a knot in the middle at the top, then take the string round again, this time at right angles to the first line, again tying it at the first knot. Keep going until the 'ball' is trussed about eight times, each time coming back to the central knot. Tuck any loose flaps of meat in as you go and close holes that might let stuffing escape.
4 Weigh the lamb.
5 Smear all over with butter. Scatter a few rosemary leaves on top.
6 Roast at 190°C/375°F/Mark 5 for 25 minutes to the pound or until the juices will run clear when the lamb is pricked with a skewer.
7 Put on a serving dish. Allow to rest for 10 minutes before carving.
8 Tip all the fat from the pan, but leave any juices. Add half a pint of water or stock to the pan and scrape any stuck sediment into the liquid as it comes to the boil. Check seasoning.
9 Carefully remove the strings before carving the lamb. Carve it as you would a cake. Serve gravy separately.

Strawberry Ring

Choux pastry

85g 3oz butter	pinch of salt
200ml ⅓pt water	3 large eggs
100g 4oz plain flour	

Filling and topping

350g 12oz strawberries	3tbsp strawberry jam
300ml ½pt double cream, whipped	250g 8oz icing sugar

1 Set oven to 200°C/400°F/Mark 6.
2 Heat butter and water together, ensuring that butter has completely melted before water boils.
3 As water boils furiously, tip in flour and salt. Remove pan from heat and immediately beat until flour is incorporated and mixture leaves sides of pan.

147

4 Allow to cool.
5 Gradually beat in two eggs and enough of the third one to give a smooth mixture which will drop, rather than run, off a spoon.
6 Spoon or pipe mixture onto a wet baking tray in a ring 25cm/10in diameter with sides approximately 2.5cm/1in high. The top and sides do not need to be smooth.
7 Bake for 25–35 minutes or until well risen, firm and brown.
8 Remove from oven, split in half horizontally. Scoop out any uncooked paste.
9 Dry inside of both halves by returning them to oven for 5–10 minutes. Allow to cool.
10 Cut strawberries into halves or quarters. Lightly fold them into the whipped cream.
11 Spread jam inside cooled bottom case and fill with strawberries and cream. Place second choux ring on top.
12 Mix icing sugar to a fairly thin consistency with a few spoons of boiling water. Spoon over ring, allowing trickles to run down sides.

MENU 42

SCALLOP AND BEAN SALAD
VEAL PARCELS
APRICOT AND PRUNE JELLY
WITH CUSTARD

Introduction

The elegant scallop salad and the rather sophisticated veal parcels with their filling of spinach and mushroom are followed by that nursery pudding – jelly and custard. But real jelly and real custard I hasten to say. First and last courses can be prepared well in advance, but the veal takes a little last minute effort.

Cook's gear

Rolling pin or meat mallet for beating out veal.

Cotton for tying veal parcels.

A decorative mould would be nice for the jelly.

Cook's tips

Frozen scallops are fine for this dish. Allow them to thaw slowly in the refrigerator. Scallops are wonderfully tender if just or barely cooked. They toughen horribly if cooked too long. Remove them from the pan as soon as they have lost their glassiness, and are just firm to the touch.

If you cannot bear to make real custard with eggs, use packet custard, but do not make it too thick, add a strip of lemon rind to the milk as you bring it to the boil, and stir in a little cream once it is made.

Getting ahead

The salad is best prepared anything up to six hours ahead of time. Do not add the dressing until the last minute.

The veal parcels can be prepared, but not cooked, in advance.

Make sure the filling and the veal are chilled before stuffing and tying, then leave loosely covered with poly-wrap for up to 24 hours. The cooking takes about 20 minutes, but the parcels will not toughen if left for half an hour in a warming drawer or very cool oven.

149

The jelly is best made between 8 and 48 hours in advance, and the custard up to 48 hours ahead – it may need whisking if it is not smooth after keeping.

Vegetable or salad?
There are beans in the salad and spinach in the veal parcels, so perhaps half-tomatoes with chopped parsley, chopped onion and bread-crumbs, sprinkled with butter and baked in the oven, would be about right. New potatoes or plain rice would provide a non-oily starch to counterbalance the fried veal.

Scallop and Bean Salad

16 scallops, fresh or frozen, sliced in half horizontally
1tbsp lemon juice
3 shallots, finely chopped
1 slice cooked ham, cut in fine strips

350g 12oz smallest French beans, cooked
350g 12oz shelled broad beans, cooked and with purplish skins removed

For the vinaigrette

2 tbsp   olive oil
1 tbsp   salad oil
1 tbsp   wine vinegar

1 tsp   finely chopped summer
    savory or thyme
salt and white pepper

1   Dress the ham and beans in vinaigrette. Arrange on eight dessert-sized plates.
2   Just before serving, stew the scallops gently for 30–40 seconds in the lemon juice with the chopped shallot until just firm and opaque.
3   Carefully arrange the scallops on top of the plates of salad and serve while still warm.

Veal Parcels

8   veal escalopes
500g   1lb   fresh spinach
175g   6oz   button
    mushrooms, finely sliced
100g   4oz   Gruyère cheese,
    cubed

4 tbsp   cream
salt and pepper
butter
lemon juice

1   Using a rolling pin, beat out the escalopes between two sheets of poly-wrap until evenly thin.
2   Wash and destalk spinach. Cook in covered pan over gentle heat until reduced in bulk but still bright green. (This requires no extra liquid if spinach leaves are still wet from being washed.)
3   Squeeze all moisture from spinach. Chop roughly.
4   Fry mushrooms in butter. Mix with spinach, cheese and cream. Season well.
5   Put a spoonful of spinach mixture onto each escalope. Wrap like a parcel and tie with cotton.
6   Fry the parcels slowly in butter until pale brown on both sides (about five minutes per side). Cover the pan and cook for further five minutes on each side. Take out and put on warm serving dish.
7   Add a squeeze of lemon juice to pan juices. Boil up and pour over veal parcels. Serve at once.

Apricot and Prune Jelly with Custard

Jelly

85g 3oz prunes	pinch of cinnamon
85g 3oz dried apricots	600ml 1pt orange juice
3tbsp sugar	2tbsp powdered gelatine

1 Soak prunes and apricots in water for 2–3 hours, then simmer gently until they are soft and the prune stones are easily removed.
2 Take out the fruit and add sugar and cinnamon to cooking liquid. Stir until sugar has dissolved.
3 Measure amount of liquid – you should have 300ml/½pt. Add water if necessary and then pour in orange juice.
4 Put six tablespoons of water into a saucepan. Sprinkle the gelatine over surface. Leave for 10 minutes and then heat gently until the gelatine has completely dissolved. Stir into the orange and prune liquid.
5 Put the prunes and apricots in the bottom of a wet jelly mould or large bowl. Pour liquid on top. Leave to set overnight in a cool place. Turn out and serve with egg custard.

Egg custard

4 egg yolks	2tsp cornflour
1tbsp caster sugar	½tsp vanilla essence
600ml 1pt creamy milk	

1 Whisk together yolks and sugar in a bowl.
2 Use a few spoons of the milk to mix the cornflour to a smooth paste in a teacup.
3 Boil the milk. Pour a little onto the cornflour paste, return to the pan and stir until boiling again. Pour from a height onto the yolks, whisking.
4 If the custard has not thickened, pour back into pan and stir over gentle heat until it does. Do not allow to boil.
5 Add vanilla.

MENU 43

MOUSSELINES DE POISSON
MUSTARD RABBIT
BLACKCURRANT KISSEL

Introduction

Rabbit haters can easily, and probably more cheaply, substitute chicken, using the same mustard recipe. If using rabbit do not risk wild ones – they can be very tough and too strong-flavoured. Hutch rabbits from the butcher are reliably young and tender. The mousselines are light and elegant and the kissel is tart, satin-smooth and extraordinarily fruity. It is also a deep dramatic purple.

Cook's gear

A good processor or mincer helps with the mousseline. For a velvet-fine texture (by no means essential) you need a hair sieve to push the fish through.

The kissel requires a similar sieve or a metal cook's sieve to extract the seeds.

Eight ramekins for the mousselines.

Cook's tips

Dijon (pale French) mustard is the best for the rabbit. Do not use English made 'French mustard' which has a dark unattractive colour and oversweet taste.

Any cheaper white fish can be substituted for the sole – haddock, cod, whiting, brill, even rock-fish, make good mousselines.

Tinned blackcurrants make kissel quite as good as fresh ones – just watch the sugar, as tinned ones are already sweetened.

Getting ahead

The mousselines can be assembled up to 24 hours ahead, or more if they are frozen raw and thawed before cooking. The base must be made ahead to allow for chilling before the cream is added.

The rabbit can be coated up to 48 hours in advance, but should be cooked just before dinner.

The kissel is best made between 8 and 24 hours ahead.

Vegetable or salad?
Plain boiled potatoes, buttered and parsleyed, are good. So are small baked ones, split and buttered. Something green (mangetout peas, runner beans?) is nice if the cook can manage that and the rabbit. Otherwise stick to salad, perhaps with a few cold cooked peas or beans among the leaves.

Mousselines de Poisson

750g 1½lb sole fillets, skinned	300ml ½pt double cream
butter for greasing	3tbsp fresh white breadcrumbs
2 egg whites	3tbsp fresh chopped parsley
2 eggs	salt, freshly ground black pepper and cayenne

To serve

1tbsp fresh chopped chives and tarragon	8tbsp single cream

1 Cut two of the fillets into four pieces each. Put the pieces between sheets of poly-wrap and beat out until large enough to cover the bottom of the ramekins. Butter the ramekins and place one piece of sole in each, skinned side up. Chill.
2 Mince the remaining fish fillets twice or pound until smooth in a food processor. Beat in the egg whites. Chill.
3 Lightly whisk the two whole eggs and stir in two tablespoons of double cream. Add the breadcrumbs and parsley, season and mix well.
4 Set oven to 200°C/400°F/Mark 6.
5 Beat the remaining double cream into the chilled fish mixture. Season well.
6 Put a layer of parsley and breadcrumb mixture into the ramekins on top of the sole fillet. Smooth the top with the back of a spoon, then fill the ramekins to just below the rim with a layer of fish mousse.
7 Stand the ramekins in a roasting tin of boiling water. Bake until the

mousses have risen slightly and are firm on top – about 15 minutes.
8   Run a knife round the edge of each mousseline and unmould onto a serving plate.
9   Season the single cream with salt and pepper and warm over low heat. Spoon over the mousselines, sprinkle with chives and tarragon and serve immediately.

Mustard Rabbit

3tbsp French mustard
3tbsp butter
juice and rind of 2 lemons

freshly ground black pepper
2 rabbits, jointed

1   Heat grill to maximum.
2   Mix mustard and other ingredients together. Spread all over rabbit joints. Leave to marinate until ready to grill.
3   Grill until very brown outside and tender inside, about 20 minutes.

Blackcurrant Kissel

1kg   2lb blackcurrants
250g 8oz caster sugar,
   possibly more

1 heaped tbsp arrowroot or
   cornflour

To serve
whipped cream or custard

1   Wash and destalk blackcurrants.
2   Put in saucepan, add sugar and barely cover with water. Simmer for 20 minutes.
3   Mix arrowroot with a little cold water to a smooth paste.
4   Add cupful of boiling fruit juice to arrowroot mixture. Stir well and then pour back into pan.
5   Simmer for 2–3 minutes, stirring.
6   When thickened push mixture through nylon or stainless steel sieve. Pour into serving bowl and cover closely with poly-wrap to prevent skin forming.
7   Serve with whipped cream or custard. (*see* recipe p. 152, Menu 42).

MENU 44

CHICKEN LIVERS AND GRAPES
PASTRY FISH
FIGS AND PEARS IN ORANGE JUICE

Introduction

The main course of this dish is very spectacular – a pastry fish, complete with scales, fins and eye. It is much simpler to do than the long recipe implies, and can be pre-prepared.

It also has the advantage that, as the fish is cooked inside the pastry crust, the flesh stays moist. Splitting the pastry releases a heady aroma of tarragon and salmon.

Cook's gear

If you want to keep large grapes whole, de-seed them with a hair-grip. Push the ends of the grip into a cork and use the curved end to hook out the grape pips from the stalk end. Then peel the grapes.

Large baking sheet (and large oven) for the fish.

Cook's tips

For the first course, if the grapes will not peel, dip them in boiling water for a few seconds. Small green seedless grapes do not need peeling.

Farmed rainbow trout is a good and considerably cheaper alternative to salmon. But any firm-fleshed, boneless fillets will do – particularly haddock, brill, turbot or grey mullet.

Sprinkling semolina on the pastry prevents the fish juices making it soggy.

Choose very ripe rather than under-ripe figs, which have no taste at all.

Getting ahead

The first course takes only about 10 minutes from start to finish. Have everything completely assembled and ready.

The fish can be prepared in advance, but should be as fresh as

156

possible. Ideally buy the fish and assemble on the morning of the party. Make the sauce in advance too, and put the fish into the oven about 45 minutes before dinner.

The fruit salad can be made a few hours ahead and kept chilled.

Vegetable or salad?

Potatoes are unnecessary with so much pastry. A rather special salad of red chicory, lamb's lettuce, or tiny mixed young salad leaves (spinach, watercress, chicory) would be perfect.

Chicken Livers and Grapes

250g   8oz large grapes
750g   1½lb cleaned chicken
   livers

85g   3oz butter
5tbsp madeira
salt and pepper
200ml   ⅓pt double cream

1   Peel and de-seed grapes.
2   Cut each piece of liver into two horizontally, to produce thin flat slices.
3   Melt butter in wide heavy frying pan. Fry livers fast, a few at a time and turning once, until firm and barely brown on the outside and still just pink inside. Lift onto warm serving dish.
4   Add grapes to pan. Shake briefly over heat. Add madeira, stir in any sediment on bottom of pan. Add salt and pepper and cream. Pour over livers.

Pastry Fish

500g   1lb puff pastry
2tbsp semolina
1.5kg   3lb salmon fillets,
   skinned
salt and black pepper

lemon juice
3 sprigs of tarragon
50g   2oz butter, chilled
1 egg, beaten

For the stock
2 slices onion
1 bay leaf
small handful of parsley
1tsp peppercorns

bones, skin and head from the
   salmon
600ml   1pt water

For the sauce

50g	2oz	butter	salt and white pepper
30g	1oz	flour	1tsp chopped fresh tarragon
3tbsp	white wine		2tbsp double cream
300ml	½pt	fish stock	

1 Set oven to 230°C/450°F/Mark 8.
2 Roll a third of the pastry into a long thin piece. Cut it roughly to the shape of a fish. Prick all over and bake for 20 minutes or until crisp. Remove from oven, allow to cool, then turn upside down and sprinkle with semolina.
3 Season the fillets with salt, pepper and lemon juice. Layer them on top of the pastry with tarragon leaves and thin slices of butter on top of each layer.
4 Roll out remaining pastry large enough to cover fish and tuck underneath cooked pastry. Lay it over the fish and, with a margin of 2.5cm/1in, cut it to shape of base pastry.
5 Gently lift the cooked pastry and fish fillets with a fish slice, tucking the raw pastry underneath to secure it.
6 Using a teaspoon mark the top of the pastry with half-circles to resemble fish scales. (Press quite deeply so that the markings still show when the pastry has been baked.)
7 Use left-over trimmings of pastry to make fins and an eye for the fish. Brush with the beaten egg.
8 Bake for 20 minutes to brown and puff up the pastry and then turn oven down to 160°C/325°F/Mark 3. Bake for further 25 minutes. Test fish with skewer to see if it is ready. There should be no resistance (other than from the pastry) to the skewer if the fish is cooked.
9 While fish is in oven, make the sauce. First boil up the stock ingredients and simmer for about 20 minutes (longer simmering of the bones produces a bitter taste). Strain.
10 Melt half the butter, add flour. Cook for few seconds. Add wine and then 300ml/½pt stock. Bring to the boil, stirring continuously. Simmer for few minutes. Add salt, pepper and tarragon. Draw off heat and beat in remaining butter. Stir in cream. Hand sauce separately.

Figs and Pears in Orange Juice

8 large fresh figs, chilled
8 small ripe pears, chilled

150ml ¼pt orange juice
1tbsp honey

1 Warm orange juice just enough to dissolve honey in it. Cool, then chill.
2 Cut each fig lengthwise into quarters. Peel and core pears and cut lengthwise into segments.
3 Put fruit in glass bowl. Pour over sweetened orange juice.

MENU 45

CAULIFLOWER AND THYME SOUP
FILO PIE
ATHOL BROSE

Introduction
This is a good dinner that can all be done the day before. Make sure the helpings of Athol Brose, which is fiendishly rich, are tiny.

Cook's gear
A liquidizer or sieve for the soup.
A paint or pastry brush for buttering the filo pie.
Very small glasses or coffee cups for serving the Athol Brose.

Cook's tips
A fine grating of nutmeg is a winter alternative to thyme in the soup.
Buy the filo pastry from a Greek delicatessen. Keep the pastry covered with poly-wrap or a damp teatowel while working or while it is waiting to go in oven, to prevent drying out.
A layer of chopped walnuts on top of the Athol Brose is good. Add them just before serving.

Getting ahead
Make the soup up to two days ahead. Keep refrigerated. Or omit the milk, freeze the cooked soup and reheat with milk.
Assemble the filo pie 24 hours in advance. Bake before serving. Or assemble well ahead, freeze unbaked. Thaw and bake on the day.
Make the Athol Brose the day before. Cover the pots or glasses with poly-wrap and keep refrigerated.

Vegetable or salad?
Make a green salad with some interesting things in it – say cooked beans or peas, diced potato, raw onion and mint in a vinaigrette dressing, to serve with the pie.

160

Cauliflower and Thyme Soup

50g   2oz butter
1 large onion, sliced
500g   1lb cauliflower florets
1tbsp flour
1 litre   2pt chicken stock

1tsp chopped fresh thyme or
   ½tsp dried thyme
300ml   ½pt creamy milk
salt and pepper

1   Melt butter. Slowly cook onion until softened. Add cauliflower. Cover. Cook gently 15–20 minutes, shaking the pan frequently to prevent burning.
2   Stir in flour.
3   Add chicken stock and thyme. Bring to boil, stirring.
4   Simmer until vegetables are soft. Liquidize.
5   Add milk. Check seasoning. Reheat without boiling.

Filo Pie

1kg   2lb minced beef
1tbsp beef dripping
2 onions, chopped
2 sticks celery, chopped
6 rashers streaky bacon, diced
1 large clove garlic, crushed
300ml   ½pt stock

2tbsp sherry, madeira or
   marsala
2tbsp tomato purée
chopped parsley
salt and pepper
250g   8oz filo pastry leaves
melted butter

1   Brown meat in half the dripping over a high heat. Remove meat.
2   Brown onion, celery, bacon and garlic – adding more fat if necessary.
3   Pour off excess fat.
4   Return meat to saucepan.
5   Add stock and alcohol. Bring to boil, stirring.
6   Add tomato purée, parsley and seasonings. Simmer until meat is tender (45 minutes).
7   Reduce sauce to syrupy consistency by boiling.
8   Check seasoning. It should be fairly peppery and strong.
9   Set oven to 200°C/400°F/Mark 6.
10 Lightly grease a shallow, ovenproof dish.
11 Lay a filo leaf in the dish, spread thinly with meat sauce. Continue the layers, finishing with filo. Brush with melted butter.
12 Add more filo leaves to top, brushing each with melted butter.
13 Bake for 30 minutes or until top is crisp and brown.

Athol Brose

600ml   1pt double cream
6tbsp runny honey
8tbsp whisky

1   Whip cream until stiff.
2   Stir in honey and whisky.
3   Spoon into individual glasses.
4   Chill.

MENU 46

DUCK LIVER AND MANGETOUT SALAD
LOBSTER WITH MUSHROOMS AND PARSLEY
CHAMPAGNE SORBET

Introduction

This menu is definitely for very keen cooks, and ones with a bit of money to spend. It is staggeringly expensive. The first course salad is fresh and pretty with an attractive combination of warm sautéed liver and crisp cold mangetout peas. The lobster preparation takes hours but the result is unbelievably good, as is the champagne sorbet.

Cook's gear

Rubber gloves for handling hot and sharp-shelled lobsters.

Hammer, mallet or lobster crackers, and lobster pick or skewer for picking out flesh from legs and claws.

Processor or liquidizer for lobster sauce.

A sorbetière or ice cream maker is not essential, but the freezer must be efficient – the ice-making compartment of a refrigerator is no good.

Cook's tips

Lobsters do not scream when dropped into boiling water, and they come with their claws rubber-banded so there is no need to fear them. But ready-boiled lobster will do too – just make sure they are freshly boiled. Order them in advance and check when the fishmonger will be buying them live. Go for medium sized creatures – the big ones are often tough and the little ones seem all shell.

White button mushrooms will discolour the sauce less than open flat ones, and their more delicate flavour will not overpower the lobster taste.

If flat-leaved parsley is not available use the curly kind, but less of it and chop it finely.

Champagne is wonderful for the sorbet but not essential – use any flowery white wine, perhaps a Riesling.

High alcohol sorbets do not freeze hard and they melt fast, so have the glasses or serving plates in the freezer before dishing up. Return to the freezer, dished up, until needed. To speed up freezing of the sorbet, have all whisks, bowls etc. well chilled before use.

If using a food processor for re-whisking, the mixture can be frozen rock-solid and simply broken into chunks and processed to smooth creaminess. Refreeze.

Getting ahead

Prepare the salad a few hours ahead, but fry the livers and add them at the last minute.

The lobsters should be bought and cooked on the day of serving. The mixture reheats well, but take care not to allow it to boil as it will toughen the lobster. Add parsley only on reheating.

The sorbet should be made between 8 hours and 5 days in advance.

Vegetable or salad?

Rice is the ideal accompaniment to the lobster, preferably plain fluffy boiled rice, very lightly buttered.

Duck Liver and Mangetout Salad

350g 12oz duck livers, trimmed of any greenish patches, diced
1tbsp oil for frying

500g 1lb mangetout peas, topped and tailed
large handful of radicchio or cos leaves

For the dressing
2tbsp mild onion or spring onion, finely chopped
3tsp lemon juice
3tsp tarragon or sherry vinegar

2tbsp salad oil
2tbsp olive oil
sait and black pepper

1 Boil the mangetouts for 3–5 minutes or until bright green and just tender. Cool immediately under cold water, drain and pat dry.
2 Combine dressing ingredients and gently coat mangetouts and salad leaves with it. Tip into a strainer so that excess dressing drains off. Arrange the salad on eight small plates.
3 Just before serving toss duck livers in hot oil for 30 seconds. They should be firm but not overcooked. Lift out with perforated spoon and lay them on top of the salads.

Lobster with Mushrooms and Parsley

2 whole cloves garlic, unpeeled
slice onion
bayleaf
stick of celery
4 1kg/2lb lobsters
100g 4oz butter

500g 1lb small white button
    mushrooms, sliced
30g 1oz flour
300ml ½pt double cream
salt and pepper
bunch of common (flat-leaved)
    parsley

To serve
boiled rice

1 Bring three pints water to the boil with garlic, onion, bayleaf and celery in it. Drop lobsters in head first, and put on a lid. Simmer for 15 minutes or until shells are bright red. Take them out and cool.

2 When cool enough to handle, split lobsters in half lengthwise. Remove thin intestinal tract running to tail, and small stomach bag (it is nearly see-through, slightly scaly and tough). Do not discard creamy greenish matter – put this into a bowl. Keep any coral too.

3 Cut tail meat into chunks and put in ovenproof dish. Add meat from inside claw shells.

4 Crush shell with a hammer or in a food processor. Put with juices and cooking liquid and simmer for 30 minutes. Strain and then boil down to 300ml/½ pint.

5 Melt half butter and gently cook mushrooms in it until reduced in size and almost all juice has evaporated. Lift the mushrooms out with perforated spoon and add them to ovenproof dish. Add any remaining juice to lobster stock.

6 Melt another ounce of butter, stir in the flour then add lobster stock. Stir until boiling then continue boiling until thick and syrupy. Add any creamy lobster from the bowl and/or coral. Liquidize.

7 Beat in last ounce of butter and the double cream. Add salt and pepper.

8 Sprinkle the parsley leaves (with thick stalks removed, but barely chopped) into the lobster dish. Pour over hot sauce, reheat briefly and serve with rice.

Champagne Sorbet

600ml	1pt	water	600ml	1pt	champagne
500g	1lb	granulated sugar	juice of 2 lemons, 1 orange		

1 Set freezer to coldest.
2 Dissolve sugar in water over gentle heat.
3 When sugar has completely dissolved boil rapidly for five minutes.
4 Add champagne and fruit juice. Allow to cool.
5 Freeze until edges are icy. Whisk until smooth. Return to freezer. Keep whisking at intervals until smooth and creamy. Keep in freezer until ready to serve.

MENU 47

TARRAGON COCOTTES
CHICKEN IN CABBAGE LEAVES
CHOCOLATE PUDDING

Introduction

The recipes of this menu are all elegant but uncomplicated.

The eggs are baked at the last minute, but they are trouble-free, the chicken can go into the oven in the serving dish half an hour before dinner, and the chocolate pudding – a kind of gourmet's blancmange – can be made well in advance.

A satisfyingly simple and good dinner.

Cook's gear

Ramekins for the eggs.

A decorative jelly mould would be nice for the pudding. If one is used, do not cover the pudding with cream but serve it separately.

Cook's tips

Accurate timing of the first course is important, so get the guests seated while the eggs are cooking, then they will not overcook while waiting to be served. If having the chicken and eggs in the oven at once is not practicable, cook the eggs standing in a roasting pan of boiling water on the cooker-top, covering the pan with foil. The eggs, if the water is bubbling, will then take about six minutes for the whites to set, leaving the yolks runny.

Buy fresh chicken breasts for the main course. If leg portions must be used, bone and skin them and cook for 10 minutes longer.

Getting ahead

Eggs can be prepared in advance – cover with poly-wrap to prevent drying out.

Chicken can be prepared for the oven in advance but is best baked immediately before dinner.

The pudding is best made 12–24 hours in advance. Cream can be whipped 24 hours ahead too.

Vegetable or salad?

Buttery potatoes such as pommes anna would be good: thinly slice potatoes, rinse and dry the slices and pack them into a buttered dish, with plenty of butter and salt and pepper.

Bake until golden on top and tender underneath. Baby carrots, or tiny turnips peeled but left whole with an 2.5cm/1in of stalk, would go well too.

Tarragon Cocottes

30g 1oz butter for greasing ramekins	8tbsp double cream
8 eggs	salt and black pepper
	chopped tarragon leaves

1 Set oven to 220°C/425°F/Mark 7.
2 Grease ramekin dishes.
3 Break an egg into each dish.
4 Add cream, salt and pepper to each one.
5 Sprinkle chopped tarragon on top.
6 Stand dishes in roasting tin two-thirds full of boiling water. Bake for 12 minutes or until whites are set but yolks are still runny.

Chicken in Cabbage Leaves

8 cabbage leaves	16 juniper berries
8 chicken breasts, skinned and boned	4 rashers of bacon, halved
salt and pepper	melted butter

1 Remove tough stalk from cabbage leaves and boil the leaves briefly.
2 Set oven to 220°C/425°F/Mark 7.
3 Season chicken breasts with salt and pepper and crushed juniper berries.
4 Place a piece of bacon on each and wrap in a cabbage leaf.
5 Brush with melted butter, place in greased ovenproof dish. Bake for 30 minutes.

Chocolate Pudding

50g   2oz cornflour
850ml   1½pt milk
300g   10oz good quality plain
   chocolate

40g   1½oz sugar
4 drops vanilla essence
200ml   ⅓pt double cream
icing sugar to taste

1   Mix cornflour with a little of the milk.
2   Heat chocolate, sugar and milk until smooth.
3   Pour onto cornflour. Mix well, return to pan. Stir until boiling, thick and smooth.
4   Add vanilla. Beat well. Allow to set in oiled pudding basin.
5   Turn out and cover with whipped cream sweetened with icing sugar.

MENU 48

LEEK TERRINE
SEAFOOD SAUSAGES
MANGO ICE CREAM

Introduction

The main course of this menu needs a good deal of time, trouble and money lavished on it. But it is spectacularly good, and the leek terrine and mango ice cream are very simple.

Cook's gear

Two identical 500g/1lb loaf tins for the terrine.

Aluminum foil for the sausages.

A processor or liquidizer to purée mangoes. A sieve may also be necessary.

A sorbetière or ice cream maker is not essential, but the freezer must be efficient – the ice-making compartment of a refrigerator is no good.

Cook's tips

To remove grit from leeks split them from the leafy end to within a few inches of the root. Riffle the ends under running water.

Take great care, and a very sharp knife, when slicing the terrine. It falls apart easily. The leeks can be served in a simple vinaigrette but the terrine-like presentation is pretty, and simple to do, providing there is space for eight plates in the refrigerator.

The cost of the main course can be greatly reduced by substituting cheaper fish for the seafood. On the other hand roasted and skinned pistachio nuts added to the fish mixture will add to the cost and to the luxury of the dish.

Any fruit purée can be substituted for the mango. Raw fruits taste purer than cooked ones, but lose their colour in the freezer after a day or two.

To speed up freezing of the ice cream, have all whisks, bowls etc. well chilled before use.

If using a food processor for re-whisking, the mixture can be frozen rock-solid and simply broken into chunks and processed to smooth creaminess. Refreeze. Repeat this process until satisfied with smooth texture of the ice cream.

Getting ahead

The leek terrine must be pressed for at least four hours and can be made the day before serving. Slice and arrange on plates a few hours in advance.

The seafood sausages can be made the day before and gently reheated in their foil jackets in fish stock or in a steamer over boiling water. The sauce can be made in advance – up to 24 hours – but because it is inclined to separate on reheating, the butter should only be beaten into it just before serving.

Make the ice cream between 12 hours and 5 days in advance.

Vegetable or salad?

White rice is essential for mopping up the sauce. Tiny crescents of baked puff pastry look pretty and are traditional but not essential. No vegetables. Follow with a simple soft-leaf salad (say Dutch butterhead lettuce) if liked.

Leek Terrine

16 leeks, cleaned
radicchio or other chicory salad
6tbsp olive oil
2tbsp wine vinegar

2tsp English mustard
85g 3oz crumbled feta or
    ricotta cheese
sea salt and black pepper

1 Remove roots and most of green part of leeks. Boil in salted water until tender. Drain.
2 Fill a loaf tin with the leeks laid lengthways – head to tail alternately.
3 Put another tin inside the first, pressing down the leeks. Invert both tins so that the water can drain out and leave for four hours with a 1kg/2lb weight on top.
4 Carefully unmould the terrine and cut into slices. Use a very sharp knife.
5 Lay each slice on a plate and surround with the salad leaves.
6 Serve with dressing made by combining remaining ingredients.

Seafood Sausages

500g 1lb fresh peeled or raw frozen shrimps or crayfish tails
500g 1lb filleted and skinned white fish, e.g. whiting

3 egg whites
600ml 1pt double cream, chilled
pinch nutmeg
salt and white pepper

For the sauce
seafood shells, fish heads, bones
1 shallot, sliced
1 bay leaf
sprigs of parsley
2tsp lemon juice
small glass white wine
1 litre 2pt water

140g 5oz butter, chilled and diced
2tsp flour
pinch cayenne pepper
salt and pepper
1tsp tomato purée

To serve
boiled white rice

1 Simmer first seven sauce ingredients to make stock. After 25 minutes, strain.
2 Mince (or beat in a processor) the raw shrimp flesh and the white fish flesh to a fine paste. Chill well.
3 Beat the egg whites (unwhisked) one by one into the mixture and chill again.
4 Just before cooking, mix the double cream, a few spoonfuls at a time, into the fish mixture. Do not overbeat or the cream will turn into butter. Season with nutmeg, salt and white pepper.
5 Butter eight 23cm × 23cm/9in × 9in pieces of foil. Put a line of fish mixture onto each one and fold or roll up carefully into a sausage shape. Bend the foil to close the ends. Lay them side by side in a roasting tin or shallow pan.
6 Reboil the stock, and pour over the fish parcels. Poach for 20 minutes (without allowing the stock to bubble). When the sausages are firm to the touch, carefully remove from the foil wrappers. Keep warm on a serving dish.
7 To make the sauce, boil the stock until it is reduced to 450ml/ ¾ pint. Melt 30g/1oz of the butter in a saucepan. Add flour and cook for 30 seconds. Add stock and stir until boiling. Season with cayenne pepper, salt, pepper and tomato purée.

8 Whisk in remaining butter pieces one by one over moderate heat. Pour over sausages and serve with hot rice.

Mango Ice Cream

3 eggs
300ml ½pt double cream
175g 6oz caster sugar

300ml ½pt milk
2 ripe mangoes
juice of 1 small lemon

1 Whisk the eggs until frothy.
2 Bring the cream, sugar and milk to the boil slowly, stirring occasionally.
3 Pour from a height onto the eggs, stirring. Allow to cool, then strain into a bowl.
4 Peel the mangoes and purée the flesh with the lemon juice. If mangoes are stringy, rub the purée through a sieve. Stir the purée into the cold custard.
5 Freeze until edges are solid but centre is still soft. Whisk until smooth. Return to freezer. Keep whisking at intervals until smooth and creamy. If mixture is too hard to scoop, remove to the refrigerator for one hour before serving.

MENU 49

CUCUMBER MOUSSE
PIGEON BREASTS WITH GRAPES AND MADEIRA
CHERRY CLAFOUTIS

Introduction

This menu is comparatively inexpensive and unusual. It does require some last minute cooking however, and a reliable butcher or game dealer who will produce young pigeon.

Cook's gear

A coarse cheese grater or julienne cutter speeds up shredding the cucumber. A ring mould would give it an attractive shape when set.

If you want to keep large grapes whole, de-seed them with a hair-grip. Push the ends of the grip into a cork and use the curved end to hook out the grape pips from the stalk end. Then peel the grapes.

The clafoutis needs a presentable tin or flan dish that can go from oven to table.

Cook's tips

The cucumber mousse contains raw cucumber and cheese, and is likely to ferment in hot weather if made more than 24 hours ahead.

If the grapes will not peel, dip them in boiling water for a few seconds. Small green seedless grapes do not need peeling.

Pigeons have huge breasts and very little else. Professional chefs generally remove the breasts and put the rest in the stock pot – a lot less trouble than trying to remove the flesh from the carcase.

Apricots, peaches, or plums make a good substitute for cherries in the clafoutis. So do rhubarb or tinned damsons.

Getting ahead

The cucumber mousse is best made between 6 and 24 hours ahead.

The pigeon dish is a last minute affair, but grapes can be peeled and the pigeon breasts browned on both sides but left raw in the middle.

174

Then last minute cooking to reheat everything and finish the pigeon will take two rather than ten minutes.

The clafoutis can be prepared ready for baking up to six hours ahead of time. It is best served warm so should be timed to come out of the oven just before dinner.

Vegetable or salad?

Almost any green vegetable would be suitable – perhaps Brussels sprouts cooked, seasoned with pepper and nutmeg, minced and mixed with white sauce or cream before reheating.

Noodles, particularly green tagliatelli, would also be good.

Cucumber Mousse

2 cucumbers, peeled
250g 8oz cream cheese
150ml ¼pt yoghurt
150ml ¼pt double cream,
    whipped
salt and black pepper

pinch of nutmeg
juice of 2 lemons
300ml ½pt chicken or
    vegetable stock
30g 1oz gelatine

1   Grate cucumbers, reserving 2.5cm/1in for decoration.
2   Oil a soufflé dish or mould.
3   Beat together cream cheese, yoghurt and cream. Mix in the cucumber, salt, pepper and nutmeg and the lemon juice.
4   Put the stock in a small saucepan. Sprinkle over the gelatine and leave for 10 minutes. Heat gently until clear – do not allow to boil.
5   Pour into cucumber mixture and mix well. Pour into mould. Chill.
6   Turn out by inverting a plate over the mould and turning the whole thing upside down, giving it a sharp shake. Decorate with slices of cucumber.

Pigeon Breasts with Grapes and Madeira

breasts from 16 young pigeons
butter for frying
500g 1lb black grapes,
    halved and seeded

4tbsp madeira
200ml ⅓pt double cream
salt and pepper

1   Fry breasts in butter until firm but still pink inside – about four minutes on each side. Remove to warm serving dish.

2   Fry grapes briefly. Add to pigeon.
3   Add madeira to pan. Boil until reduced to one tablespoon. Mix in cream, pour over pigeon and grapes. Grind salt and pepper over top. Serve at once.

Cherry Clafoutis

1 large tin pitted Morello cherries, well drained

butter for greasing dish
icing sugar for top

For batter
50g   2oz flour
pinch of salt
2tbsp caster sugar
4 whole eggs

3 egg yolks
600ml   1pt creamy milk
1tbsp brandy, sherry, or kirsch

1   Set oven to 190°C/375°F/Mark 5.
2   Butter large shallow flan dish. Spread cherries evenly over base.
3   Liquidize batter ingredients until smooth. Pour over cherries.
4   Bake until puffed up and brown (about 45 minutes). Allow to cool to lukewarm. Dust heavily with icing sugar.

MENU 50

TWICE BAKED SOUFFLÉ
CHICKEN IN SHARP SAUCE
RASPBERRIES AND GRAPES

Introduction

A soufflé that is deliberately allowed to sink and a chicken cooked in vinegar with a handful of garlic cloves do sound unpromising, but both recipes are exceptionally good. The soufflé method is a foolproof way of ensuring a risen but moist production. The soufflés are very rich in eggs and cheese. Do not offer second helpings. The curious ingredients and unusual cooking method for the chicken produce an astonishingly subtle and delicious dish.

Cook's gear

Small ovenproof teacups or dariole moulds for the cheese soufflés.
Ramekins will do, but they produce rather flat soufflés.

Cook's tips

Do not attempt to unmould the soufflés until they have cooled to tepid. They are then firmer and easier to handle.

Do not wash the raspberries unless absolutely necessary. Just tip them straight onto the guests' plates or into a glass serving bowl. Try to avoid serving cream with the dessert; the rest of the dinner contains rather a lot of it.

A few of the grapes, kept in tiny bunches and dipped first in unbeaten egg white and then in caster sugar, look pretty on top of the fruit.

Getting ahead

The soufflés are best given their first baking up to eight hours before dinner. The final reheating, of course, must be done just before serving.

Do not freeze or make the chicken dish too far in advance. It can be cooked on the afternoon of the dinner, and the sauce completed.

Reheat the chicken pieces in the oven, then pour over the sauce and add the chervil and tomato strips when dishing up.

The raspberries need no preparation beyond chilling. The grapes can be washed and the stalks removed some time on the day of the dinner.

Vegetable or salad?

Mashed potato, or better still floury potatoes put through a mincer so that the threads of potato fall directly into the serving dish, would be not too rich, but absorbent enough to mop up the sauce. Reheat in a low oven. A clean uncomplicated green vegetable (tiny peas perhaps, or runner beans) would be best.

Twice Baked Soufflé

450ml ¾pt milk	275g 9oz strong Cheddar
slice of onion	cheese, grated
pinch of nutmeg	6 eggs, separated
85g 3oz butter	450ml ¾pt creamy white
85g 3oz flour	sauce
pinch of dry English mustard	salt and pepper

1 Set oven to 190°C/375°F/Mark 5. Butter insides of eight ovenproof teacups.
2 Heat milk slowly with onion and nutmeg. Remove onion.
3 Melt butter, stir in flour and mustard.
4 Add milk, off heat, whisking until smooth. Return to heat, bring to boil, stirring.
5 When thickened, remove from heat, add 250g/8oz of the cheese. Stir in egg yolks. Check seasoning.
6 Whisk egg whites until stiff. Fold into cheese mixture.
7 Two-thirds fill teacups with mixture. Stand in roasting tin of boiling water. Bake for 15–20 minutes or until set. Allow to sink and cool.
8 Loosen soufflés and turn out into a buttered ovenproof dish.
9 To serve: heat oven to 240°C/475°F/Mark 8. Sprinkle remaining cheese over top of soufflés and coat them with the sauce seasoned with salt and pepper.
10 Bake for 15 minutes or until risen and brown. Serve promptly.

Chicken in Sharp Sauce

16 chicken pieces
50g 2oz butter
8 large garlic cloves, unpeeled
6tbsp wine vinegar
450ml ¾pt dry white wine
3tbsp brandy
3tsp pale French mustard

2tsp tomato purée
450ml ¾pt very fresh double
  cream
salt and pepper
3 tomatoes, peeled and seeded
sprigs of chervil

1 Brown chicken pieces in butter, skin side first. Add unpeeled garlic. Cover pan, cook over low heat for 20 minutes or until chicken is tender.
2 Pour off all but a tablespoon of fat. Add vinegar to the chicken in the pan, mixing well with the sediment on bottom. Boil rapidly until liquid has reduced to two tablespoons. Put chicken in warm dish.
3 Add wine, brandy, mustard and tomato purée to pan. Boil for 5 minutes or until thick and syrupy.
4 Boil the cream in a small, heavy-bottomed pan, stirring frequently, until reduced by half. Sieve the vinegar sauce into the cream, pressing the garlic to extract the pulp.
5 Check seasoning of the sauce. Pour it over the chicken pieces. Cut the tomatoes into strips and scatter over top with the chervil sprigs.

Raspberries and Grapes

1kg 2lb raspberries

1kg 2lb seedless grapes

In a large shallow glass bowl gently mix together raspberries and destalked tiny seedless grapes. Chill.

MENU 51

MUSSEL SOUP
DUCK AND VEGETABLE PANCAKES
ORANGES WITH VAN DER HUM

Introduction

This menu requires duck legs – something not easily bought except on a whole duck. But it is designed for cooks who have used duck breasts only to make the main dish of menu 22, and have prudently frozen the legs for future use. Of course meat from the whole duck would do. The mussel soup is troublesome to make but always successful, and the orange salad is light and fresh to finish with.

Cook's gear

A liquidizer or sieve is essential for a velvet-smooth soup, and would speed up making pancake batter.

A sharp serrated knife is vital for neatly peeling and slicing the oranges.

Cook's tips

Fresh mussels undoubtedly make the best soup. If you do buy tinned ones, however, make sure they are packed in water or brine, not vinegar, which is more usual, but totally unsuitable for soup.

The orange salad calls for the tangerine-based liqueur Van der Hum, but any orange-based liqueur (Cointreau, Curaçao, Grand Marnier) would do, or indeed the liqueur can be left out altogether for a less rich salad.

Getting ahead

The mussel soup can be made up to 48 hours in advance and kept refrigerated. Take care not to boil on reheating, and add cream at the last minute.

The pancakes can be made up to 24 hours in advance and kept,

180

wrapped in a cloth, in the refrigerator. Fill and heat before dinner.

The orange salad is best made up to 12 hours in advance and chilled.

Vegetable or salad?

Somehow vegetables do not go with pancakes, and more starch in the form of rice or potatoes would be a mistake. Just follow with a crisp herby green salad with oil and vinegar dressing.

Mussel Soup

2kg 4lb fresh live mussels	2 onions, finely chopped
2 glasses white wine	nutmeg
600ml 1pt water	85g 3oz flour
bay leaf, parsley, stick of celery, thyme sprigs	600ml 1pt milk
	salt and black pepper
85g 3oz butter	300ml ½pt single cream

1 Soak mussels in fresh water to remove sand. Scrub shells to remove 'beards'. Discard any open or cracked ones.
2 Put cleaned mussels in large saucepan with wine. Cover and cook over high heat for 4–5 minutes. Open the pan and check the mussels have opened. If not, cover and give them a few more minutes.
3 Keep pan juices. Discard any unopened mussels. Remove mussels

from shells – but keep the shells. Cover the mussels and put to one side.

4 Add shells, water, bay leaf, parsley, celery, and thyme to saucepan with wine and juices. Bring to boil and simmer for 10 minutes.

5 In separate pan, melt butter, add onion and nutmeg and cook until onion is soft. Stir in flour. Cook for one minute.

6 Strain liquid from first saucepan into onions, taking care to leave behind any sand. Whisk as the soup comes to the boil and thickens.

7 Add mussels and milk. Reheat gently without boiling. Sieve or liquidize. Check seasoning and stir in cream.

Duck and Vegetable Pancakes

250g 8oz carrots
250g 8oz cucumber
1 small green pepper
50g 2oz butter

salt and pepper
2tbsp lemon juice
8 duck legs, roasted

Pancake batter
250g 8oz plain flour
pinch of salt
2 eggs
2 egg yolks

600ml 1pt milk or milk and
     water mixed
2tbsp oil

1 Put all batter ingredients into liquidizer and blend until smooth. Leave to stand for half an hour and then make 16 medium sized, very thin pancakes. Stack them on a plate.

2 Cut all the vegetables into fine matchsticks about 5cm/2in long.

3 Melt butter and in it soften the vegetables over low heat. Season with salt, pepper and a little lemon juice.

4 Remove duck meat from bone. Discard skin and slice meat into strips.

5 Divide duck and vegetables between the pancakes. Roll up and place in ovenproof dish. Brush with melted butter.

6 Heat grill to maximum and place pancakes underneath. Grill until crisp on top and heated through. Or reheat in a hot oven.

Oranges with Van Der Hum

16 oranges   8tbsp Van der Hum
caster sugar

1   With a serrated knife, peel the oranges as you would an apple,
    removing all traces of pith with the skin.
2   Slice the oranges and remove any pips.
3   Sprinkle with sugar and pour liqueur over slices. Chill.

MENU 52

FILO EGGS
RACK OF LAMB WITH MUSTARD AND MINT
PEAR CREAMS

Introduction

The fried egg starter is at the same time dramatic and simple, but does require the sort of flat or house where the smell of frying does not drift everywhere. The lamb is plain but good, and the pear creams are really a simple nursery fool.

Cook's gear

A deep-fryer or a wide deep frying pan is essential for the first course.

Processor, liquidizer or vegetable mill to purée pears.

Small glasses, cups or large ramekins are needed for the pear cream, which is too sloppy to dish up from a central bowl.

Cook's tips

Keep filo pastry covered with poly-wrap or brush the sheets with butter while working or when waiting for the next stage, otherwise they dry out and become too brittle to handle.

Make sure the oil is very clean. Dark oil smells horrible and gives a dark coat to the food. Wear a shower-cap or scarf knotted like a turban to keep the smell of frying out of your hair.

Serve lamb pink if possible, rather than cooked to uniform greyness. If well done lamb is wanted, a roast shoulder would be cheaper and juicier than best end. If using best end, ask the butcher to trim the bones in the French way – cutting away nine-tenths of the fat and scraping between the bones (which should be cut off short) so that each bone is seen separately – as he would for a crown of lamb.

Getting ahead

The eggs can be prepared a few hours in advance of cooking, but they must be fried just before dinner.

184

Prepare lamb ahead but do not cook until just before dinner.

Pear creams are best made the day before and kept tightly covered with poly-wrap.

Vegetable or salad?

Tiny roast potatoes would be very good, but they seldom come out perfectly. Hedge your bets and sauté them: boil or steam small potatoes in their skins. When cooked, peel them. Fry gently and carefully on all sides in butter to a pale brown.

Put them in the oven, with a sprig of rosemary, to reheat just before the lamb is done. Peas are good with lamb too. If you want only one vegetable dish to handle, boil new potatoes with mint and when they are nearly cooked add young fresh or frozen peas, boil five minutes, then drain them both together and butter lightly.

Filo Eggs

4 sheets filo pastry
50g 2oz melted butter
2tbsp onion, finely chopped
2tbsp chopped parsley

8 small eggs
sea salt and black pepper
oil for frying
2 lemons, quartered

1 Cut filo into eight rectangles 20 × 20cm/8 × 8in.
2 Place each pastry sheet on a saucer. The edges will hang over the saucer rim. Brush edges with melted butter.
3 In the dip in the centre put ½ teaspoon each of chopped onion and chopped parsley.
4 Break an egg into each saucer. Season with salt and pepper. Fold over the edges of pastry and seal them together by pressing gently, and painting with melted butter, to make small parcels.
5 Fry for 30 seconds on each side in very hot oil. They will puff up and brown. Drain on absorbent paper.
6 Serve at once, with the lemon quarters handed separately.

Rack of Lamb with Mustard and Mint

5tbsp pale French mustard or
   2tbsp English mustard
2tbsp fresh mint, chopped
4tbsp fresh parsley, chopped

salt and pepper
4 6-bone best ends lamb
4tbsp fresh white breadcrumbs
2tbsp melted butter

1   Set oven to 220°C/425°F/Mark 7.
2   Mix mustard, herbs and seasonings.
3   Spread lamb with mixture.
4   Press breadcrumbs over rounded side and sprinkle with butter.
5   Roast, crumbed side up, for 40 minutes or until brown on top and pink inside. If using two roasting tins, change them from top to bottom half way through the cooking time.

Pear Creams

4 large ripe pears
1tbsp caster sugar
200ml   ⅓pt double cream

200ml   ⅓pt thickish custard
   (from a packet is fine)
2tbsp runny honey
juice of ½ a lemon

1   Peel, core and purée the pears. Sweeten if necessary.
2   Whip the cream.
3   Beat pear purée into custard. Fold in cream. Pour into ramekins. Chill.
4   Heat honey gently with lemon juice until smooth. Cool, then pour a thin glaze over each pear cream.

INDEX

Chablis sauce, 93
Champagne sorbet, 166
Cheese and sorrel soufflé, 103
Cheesecake, cinnamon, 22–3
Cherry
  clafoutis, 176
  strudel, 94
Chestnut roll, 54
Chicken
  breasts with ricotta and spinach,
    60
  cooling, 123
  coq au vin blanc, 114–15
  curry with yoghurt, 90
  in cabbage leaves, 168
  in sharp sauce, 179
  liver and croûton salad, 92
  livers with grapes, 157
  paprika, 15–16
  poulet au riz, 124–5
  Riesling, 32–3
  smitane, 68
Chocolate
  coated ice cream, 128–9
  frozen white cream, 108
  profiteroles, 72
  pudding, 169
  sauce, 108
Choux pastry, 147–8
Cinnamon cheesecake, 22–3
Clams 52
  chowder, 53
Coeurs à la creme, 118
Coffee soufflé, 135
Consommé, jellied, with mock
  caviare, 36
Coq au vin blanc, 114–15
Coriander and mushroom pâté, 39
Cream with sweetbreads and
  calvados, 131–2
Crème patissière, 111–12
Cucumber
  and caraway, 110
  and smoked trout pâté, 137

mousse, 175
  with yoghurt and mint, 127
Cumin
  carrot and mushroom salad, 107
  with iced borscht, 21
Curry chicken with yoghurt, 90
Custard, 152

Date and mango salad, 87
Daube à la Provençale, 9
Dill with Swedish lamb, 25–6
Duck
  and vegetable pancakes, 182
  breasts with green peppercorns,
    82
  choosing, 62
  liver and mangetout salad, 164
  marmalade, 127–8
  with blackcurrants and port,
    64–5

Eggs
  Arnold Bennett, 74
  filo, 185
  omelette salad, 15
  tapenade, 85

Fat, to remove from sauces, 7
Figs and pears in orange juice, 159
Filo pastry, 11
  eggs, 185
  lamb cutlets in, 13
  pie, 161
Fish
  baked grey mullet with herbs, 36
  Japanese raw salmon with lime,
    12
  kipper fillet salad, 134
  mousselines de poisson, 154–5
  pastry, 157–8
  quenelles with Chablis sauce, 93
  roast carp with peppers, 107–8
  turbot seafood kebabs, 19
Flan, fresh fruit, 43–4